Satan Goes to the
Mind Control Convention

Manchurian Candidates, Recovered Memories,
and the Dark Side of Conspiracy Culture

(and other stories)

by

Joseph L. Flatley

JOSEPH L. FLATLEY PRESS
PITTSBURGH

Satan Goes to the Mind Control Convention: Manchurian Candidates, Recovered Memories, and the Dark Side of Conspiracy Culture by Joseph L. Flatley

Published by Joseph L. Flatley Press

The author can be contacted through his website: lennyflatley.net

ISBN-13: 978-1727535563
ISBN-10: 1727535561

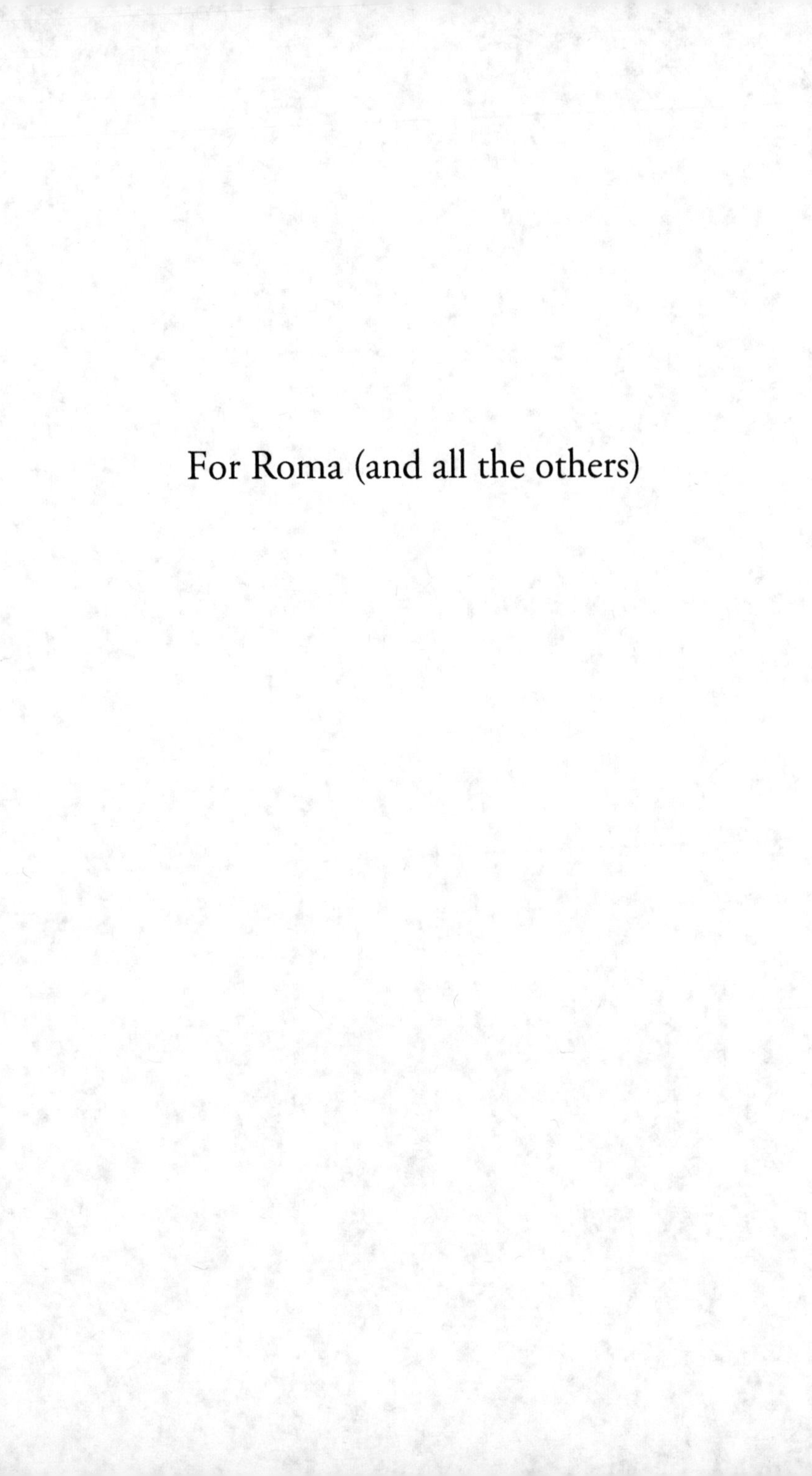

For Roma (and all the others)

CONTENTS

I believe that what destabilized Danny was an extremely
virulent strain of the information virus we're suffering from
collectively as a nation: Conspiracy Theory Fever. A slow-
acting virus that has infected our ability to know the truth
about the secret history of our age.
— Ron Rosenbaum, *The Secret Parts of Fortune*

A total absence of illusions is the mark of an empty and
constricted existence.
— Stanley H. Teitelbaum, *Illusion and Disillusionment:
Core Issues in Psychotherapy*

INTRODUCTION

An early draft of this book began with the following:

> **Author's Note:** Throughout this work, I refer to "conspiracy theorists" and "conspiracy theories," mostly (if not always) in the pejorative sense. By conspiracy *theories*, I am strictly talking about unproven or unprovable ideas that are believed in absence of evidence. By conspiracy *theorists*, I am referring to the community that has developed around these fringe ideas. I wouldn't use the words "conspiracy theory" and "conspiracy theorist" at all if there were better terms for what I'm trying to discuss. Unfortunately, there are not.

I'm not entirely sure what the point of that note was. I guess I was trying to have it both ways—trying to appeal to the people who scoff at conspiracy theories, while at the same time telling the proud conspiracy theorists that they were still welcome to enjoy this book. In effect, I was saying: "I'm not talking about you. You're cool. I'm talking about the *other* conspiracy theorists, the crazy ones."

This is a book about conspiracy theories. In the first part, "Satan Goes to the Mind Control Convention," I attempt to crash a meeting of mental health professionals who believe in things like reincarnation, alien abduction, and CIA mind control plots. The second part of the book examines the "virtual reality" that one often finds themselves in once they radically challenge consensus reality. You'll meet someone who claims that the terrorist attack on the Boston Marathon was little more than Hollywood special effects; a man who looks at the world and sees a large, spinning disc; and an online community of people who have convinced themselves that they're being surveilled by an out-of-control government. And of course, you will meet people who have turned these beliefs into thriving businesses. You'll also meet the man who killed 11 people in my hometown of Pittsburgh because he believed that they were a threat to the white race.

Thanks to the internet, I am able to pinpoint exactly what ignited my interest in conspiracy theories in the first place: the July/August 1992 issue of the LA punk zine *Flipside*.[1] Odd for a music magazine—but perfectly in tune with the "anything goes" ethos of punk—this issue featured an interview with the professional conspiracy theorist William Cooper. That man was *out there*. He pushed a paranoid version of Christianity that placed the true believers of Christ on one side of an eternal battle with Lucifer, as embodied by the Freemasons and the United Nations. Sure, in retrospect it was all Glenn Beck's

Chalkboard stuff, but at the time I was mesmerized.

It was also around this time that I discovered Robert Anton Wilson, the self-described "agnostic mystic." He explored the same topics as William Cooper, but with a skepticism and humor that seemed to elude most conspiracy theorists, who were (as far as I could tell) predominantly paranoid and right-wing and unable to take a joke.

You might say that I laughed at William Cooper, but I laughed *with* Robert Anton Wilson.

In his book *The Cosmic Trigger*, Wilson recounts a series of mystical experiences that resulted from what he termed "a process of deliberately induced brain change . . . called 'initiation' or 'vision quest' in many traditional societies."[2] Whether attempted through psychedelic drugs or yoga or some other method, this sort of thing has the potential to leave one very unsure of where reality ends and fantasy begins.

In describing his mindset after years of psychic experimentation, Wilson invokes Chapel Perilous, from Sir Thomas Malory's *Morte D'Arthur*.

"In researching occult conspiracies," Wilson writes, "one eventually faces a crossroad of mythic proportions (called Chapel Perilous in the trade). You come out the other side either a stone paranoid or an agnostic; there is no third way." Ultimately, you can only hope to escape Chapel Perilous "if you are armed with the wand of intuition, the cup of sympathy, the sword of reason and the pentacle of valor."

In the legend cited by Wilson, the four suits of the Tarot deck indicate the four qualities that are necessary to escape Chapel Perilous and complete the hero's journey.

There are lessons to be learned from this, even if you're not the type to involve yourself in an "initiation" or "vision quest." Intuition, sympathy, reason, valor: these are all qualities that enable us to see more of the world as it is, as opposed to what we hope (or fear) it might be.

This is why I'm fascinated by conspiracy theories, and why I think they are worthy of serious investigation. Conspiracy theorists represent the breakdown that occurs either when the information needed to be an informed citizen is unavailable, or when one is overwhelmed by events, or when one lacks the ability to understand what is in front of them. For the conspiracy theorist—for all of us, probably—the "present shock" of the digital age and the implosion of civil society have transformed American life into a sort of Chapel Perilous. In these pages, I offer several examples of what this means on a practical level.

Of course, by "conspiracy theorist," I'm not referring to you; I mean all those *other* kooks out there.

SATAN GOES TO THE MIND CONTROL CONVENTION

PREFACE

In the spring of 2018, I traveled to Chicago for the annual conference of the International Society for the Study of Trauma and Dissociation (ISST-D), an organization for mental health professionals founded in 1984. The event was held at the historic Palmer House Hilton Hotel, in Chicago's Loop, a few blocks from Lake Michigan. The 25-story Beaux Arts structure dates back to the 1920s and boasts "a two-story, gilded lobby with a formal staircase, marble-topped tables, velvet seating, and a ceiling mural depicting Greek mythology" for "the ultimate in luxury," according to *Historic Hotels of America.*[3] The Palmer House location gave an air of respectability to the conference that it might have lacked at something less upscale but more apropos, like an airport Quality Inn.

Members of the ISST-D promote recovered memory therapy (RMT), an unconventional and controversial type of therapy that is largely discredited in the mainstream mental health community.[*] According to its critics, the

---

[*] According to Ofshe and Watters, recovered memories of child abuse fall into three categories: recovered memories of abuse that happened

ISST-D is little more than a clearinghouse for mental health quackery.

Recovered memory therapists often believe that their patients possess multiple personalities. Once called multiple personality disorder, this condition is now known as dissociative identity disorder,[4] though the two terms are used interchangeably. In the medical community, the existence of DID has largely been discredited, although it's still widely believed in popular culture.

"Those with this diagnosis of multiple personality disorder learn to accept that they embody dozens or hundreds of separate personalities," write Ofshe and Watters in *Making Monsters*, "each with its own memory and set of experiences."[5]

RMT didn't develop in a vacuum. During the 1980s and 1990s, the United States experienced a moral panic that adopted the therapy as "scientific" proof of its claims. Dubbed the "Satanic Panic," this was a movement, mostly by evangelical Christian groups, that saw Satan as the B-Movie villain behind any number of social ills, including child abuse, teen suicide, drug use, *Dungeons and Dragons*, and heavy metal music. This was big on the Christian seminar circuit, and soon mainstream America came to believe that Satan worshippers posed a threat to its children. Through "cult training," a generation of teachers, cops, and social workers were told that Satanists had been

when the person was a child, people who believe they were abused at the hands of a cult, and people who come to believe they have multiple personalities. Ofshe and Watters, *Making Monsters* pp. 1-2 incorporating child abuse in their rituals for generations (this was called "ritual abuse," or sometimes "Satanic ritual abuse"). Unscrupulous therapists were able to draw out false memories from people who had no idea that they'd been abused until they'd encountered the idea of "recovered memories" in therapy or in the media. People seeking help for mundane complaints like depression and anxiety were told that their problems were caused by "repressed" ritual abuse, and that only recovered memory therapy could make this right. Turning Freud's maxim on its head, recovered memory therapists went to work transforming "common unhappiness" into "hysterical misery."*

The Satanic Panic accomplished a few things. It gave Americans a concrete (and literal) devil to fear. It also created an epidemic of dissociative identity disorder diagnoses; according to a legal survey conducted by an organization called the False Memory Syndrome Foundation, the group had collected "well over 1,800 records of litigation related to repressed memory claims" by 1998.[6]

It wasn't only Satanic Panic true-believers who were swept up in this hysteria. There are a few well-known instances where so-called Satanists were accused of crimes and suffered greatly for it. In the West Memphis Three case, a group of teenagers spent 18 years in prison after being

---

* The whole point of therapy, according to Freud, is to "[turn] your hysterical misery into common unhappiness." Sigmund Freud, *Studies on Hysteria* (1895)

convicted of the murder of three young boys in West Memphis, Arkansas. They were accused not because there was any evidence, but because they were into heavy metal music and at least one of them owned books by British occultist Aleister Crowley. The West Memphis Three were finally released in 2011, and the real killer has never been brought to justice.[7]

In 1983 in Manhattan Beach, a well-to-do neighborhood in southwest Los Angeles County, a woman named Judy Johnson told the police that she believed her son had been abused by an employee of his preschool named Ray Buckey. This led to a police investigation that spread panic among the other parents of the school, and soon a number of students were making claims of abuse that ran the gamut from shocking (child pornography and slaughtered animals)[8] to absurd (Chuck Norris was named as one of the perpetrators of the abuse).[9] It only took the longest and most expensive trial in history (at the time), but eventually, all charges against Ray Buckey were dismissed, and his mother Peggy McMartin Buckey was found innocent of all charges.[10] Ultimately, it was never determined that Judy Johnson's son—or anybody's child, for that matter—had ever been abused by anybody at the McMartin preschool, at all.

For a while, talk of Satanic ritual abuse was very much in the mainstream—the 1980s saw a great deal of local news coverage of Satanic abuse allegations, and by the early 1990s, Geraldo Rivera, Sally Jessy Raphael, Oprah Winfrey, and *20/20* had all broadcast episodes with names like "Devil

Worship: Exploring Satan's Underground" and "Child Sacrifice" and "Baby Breeders." By the end of the 1990s, most Americans were no longer taking the threat of a Satanic cult underground seriously. Even Geraldo came to see the error of his ways. "I am convinced that I was terribly wrong," he said on his show, *Rivera Live*. "Many innocent people were convicted and went to prison" because of the Satanic Panic, "and I am equally positive [that the] 'Repressed Memory Therapy Movement' is also a bunch of crap. . ."[11]

While recovered memory and Satanic abuse myths lost their mainstream appeal, both became mainstays of Conspiracy Theory culture.

In *A Culture of Conspiracy: Apocalyptic Visions in Contemporary America*, political scientist Michael Barkun pinpointed the bizarre marriage of far-right-wing politics and UFO beliefs that largely defines contemporary conspiracy theory. "Throughout the 1990s," he wrote, "the right-wing conspiracy theories increasingly came together with beliefs about visiting creatures from outer space."[12] Even Timothy McVeigh, in the run-up to the Oklahoma City bombing, paid a visit to Area 51, to see if he could document evidence of UFOs.[13]

When Barkun's book came out in 2003, these fringe beliefs seemed destined to remain fringe beliefs. In the years since, we have had our first millionaire conspiracy celebrity (Alex Jones),[14] our first conspiracy president (Donald Trump),[15] and the normalization of conspiracy tropes in general. These days, no national tragedy, from the Boston

Bombing to Sandy Hook, can happen without a vocal segment of the population claiming it was a hoax staged by elites for political gain.[16] And now, the president's base is starting to embrace QAnon,[*] one of the more absurd conspiracy theories out there.[17] This can only signal the far-right's further disengagement from reality. If (when) a demagogue takes full advantage of this state of affairs, whatever's left of democracy in this country doesn't stand a chance.

And it's all there in the recovered memory movement: the shadowy cabal of child abusers with ties to the CIA, or the New World Order, or extraterrestrial beings, or all three; the abandonment of science for pseudoscience; the abdication of common sense; the odious political agenda. RMT is a marriage of psychotherapy and conspiracy, a development that has largely gone unnoticed in the mainstream.

When I went to Chicago, I expected to discover a throwback to the Satanic Panic of the 1980s and 1990s. Instead, I found a window into a frighteningly possible future.

---

* This conspiracy theory centers around an anonymous individual known only as Q. Since October 2017, they've been posting supposed "leaks" from the White House that indicate what's *really* going on behind the scenes. This internet-based phenomenon recently made the jump to real life, with Trump supporters waving "Q" signs at rallies. The danger here is that a population sufficiently whipped up by Q could be manipulated by a dishonest politician, or someone who is trying to gain political power.

1

I was leaving my neighborhood public library when I spotted three nervous librarians standing in a circle, passing a book back and forth among them like it was radioactive. I heard one of them say something about Interlibrary Loan. They were joking, but they also seemed a little freaked out. I had a hunch I knew what the book was, so I asked: "Is it about Satanism? I mean, is Satan in the title?"

As it turned out, my hunch was correct. The book was titled *Satanic Ritual Abuse: Principles of Treatment*, and its author was Colin A. Ross, M.D. I had been waiting for it to come through Interlibrary Loan for at least two weeks.

I've been reading a lot of dry textbooks on strange topics recently. In addition to *Satanic Ritual Abuse*, there is Colin Ross's *Multiple Personality Disorder: Diagnosis, Clinical Features, Treatment* and Frank W. Putnam's *Diagnosis and Treatment of Multiple Personality Disorder*, and *The Sexual Exploitation of Children: A Practical Guide to Assessment, Investigation, and Intervention* by Seth L. Goldstein. This last book is a black hardcover, decorated by a diabolical child's drawing in red crayon. If that weren't creepy enough, this edition is a misprint. The cover is upside-down and backward, which I suspect would really freak people out if I were ever caught reading it in public. Which will never happen. I keep it on the top shelf of tall a bookcase, with the spine towards the back, so that my fourth grader won't find it.

I was at the library to print out a Greyhound ticket I'd purchased online. Early the next morning I'd be on a bus bound for Chicago; I had learned that Colin Ross was scheduled to speak at a conference for mental health professionals, and that something called The Satanic Temple had announced its intention to protest the event. The combination of Ross—who writes books on things like Satanic Ritual Abuse and CIA mind control experimentation—and the Satanists (*hey, they're Satanists!*) sounded too strange to pass up.

The conference was organized by the International Society for the Study of Trauma and Dissociation. At first glance, the ISST-D seems legit; it offers research grants, classes, and continuing education credits for mental health professionals,[18] and according to its IRS 990 forms brings in around half a million dollars in program service revenue each year.[19] But if you look closely at the organization, that legitimacy becomes questionable.

The ISST-D was founded in 1984 as the International Society for the Study of Multiple Personality Disorder, but the name of the organization changed after the American Psychological Association rechristened multiple personality disorder (MPD) as dissociative identity disorder (DID).[20] Everybody I've spoken to for this story uses these two names interchangeably, although I'll be using DID whenever possible to keep up-to-date.

Bennett Braun, one of the group's founders and a past president, had to pay a $10.6 million settlement to a woman named Patricia Burgus after she accused him of using hypnosis and psychiatric medications to convince her she "possessed 300 personalities, ate human flesh, and sexually abused her two sons," according to *Chicago* magazine.[21] *New City Chicago* reported in June 1995 that "Braun played a key role in defining the modern approach to MPD."[22] Upon diagnosing his first instance of the disorder in 1974, Braun "went on to become a leading clinician in the field."

Another influential member of the ISST-D was D. Corydon Hammond, a professor at the University of Utah School of Medicine. Hammond is a past president of both the International Society for Neurofeedback and Research and the American Society of Clinical Hypnosis.[23] He's well known in conspiracy circles because of a speech he gave to the Fourth Annual Eastern Regional Conference on Abuse and Multiple Personality Disorder in 1992.[24] In the "Greenbaum Speech," Hammond claims that "very organized" cults "with interstate communication" roam the country, using their "very, very systematic brainwashing" technology on unsuspecting victims. He ties Greenbaum to the very real Operation Paperclip, a secret American government intelligence program that brought Nazi scientists into the United States following World War II. According to journalist Annie Jacobsen, "Under Operation Paperclip, which began in May of 1945, the scientists who helped the Third Reich wage war continued their weapons-related work for the U.S. government, developing rockets, chemical and biological weapons, aviation and space medicine (for enhancing military pilot and astronaut performance), and many other armaments at a feverish and paranoid pace that came to define the Cold War."[25] Hammond claims the Nazi scientists taught mind control techniques to someone named Greenbaum, a Hasidic Jew and a fan of Aleister Crowley, who then passed this information on to the United States government.

But it was Colin Ross, a former president of the ISST-D, who interested me the most. He was unapologetic in his theories about CIA mind control and Satanic conspiracies, even if he couched these strange beliefs in a dry, academic style. I also hoped that Ross could get me into the conference. The ISST-D seems to be media shy; I'd contacted them a few times in the weeks leading up to the event, and each time they'd given me the brush off. I hoped that having a former ISST-D president vouch for me might finally get me some sort of access.

Ross was scheduled to present a panel called "The Impact of the 'Memory Wars' on the Trauma Field and the ISST-D." The "Memory Wars" refers to a period spanning the 1980s and 1990s when scientists, therapists, and the justice system were drawn into a furious debate about the nature of memory, mainly because courts were seeing more cases in which adults claimed that they'd "repressed" memories of child abuse for decades, only to have them "recovered" with the help of therapists years after the fact.

It was at this time that the terms "false memories" and "recovered memories" came into use. Really, these are two different ways to respond to the same phenomenon. Since the beginning of psychoanalysis, therapists have known that if you go digging around in somebody's psyche—using hypnosis, dream analysis, word association, or ether, for instance—you're liable to uncover some weird shit.[*] The Memory Wars centered on the nature of these experiences: were they recalling actual events, or were they elaborate fantasies implanted in the memories of suggestible patients by incompetent therapists?[26]

According to proponents of recovered memory therapy, people can have memories locked in their mind somewhere, which can subsequently become unlocked and played back, fully formed, like a hidden track on a CD. It's theorized that these memories become repressed as a result of extreme trauma, and that the existence of repressed memories is itself evidence of extreme trauma.

On the other side of the debate is a group called the False Memory Syndrome Foundation. Founded in 1992 by

[*] "The appearance of occult and pseudo-telepathic subjective events in psychoanalysis has been documented, and similar phenomena are common in [Scientology]. . . . And the same therapy that produced these uncanny phenomena also stimulated a will to believe. In psychoanalytic language, one might say that patients in any intensive analytic therapy *regress*." Bainbridge, *Satan's Power*, pp. 56-57

Peter and Pamela Freyd after their adult daughter accused Peter of sexual assault (memories of which had been "repressed" her entire adult life, until they were suddenly "recovered" years after the fact), the FMSF is an advocacy group for parents accused of assault on the basis of recovered memories.[27] According to the FMSF, which boasts "a stellar board of scientific advisers," memory isn't hidden and then recovered during RMT. The experience of having these memories is real, of course, but the memories themselves are implanted. According to this school of thought, memory is seen more as an activity, something done just as easily with real events as with events suggested by shrinks or cops, or pretty much anyone else in authority.

And if all that isn't weird enough, recovered memories of abuse often entail rituals conducted by Satanists (or, some have theorized, by CIA agents pretending to be Satanists). This is where the recovered memory field gets the acronym SRA: Satanic ritual abuse.

The recovered memory therapists claim that when abuse is brutal enough, the victim's personality splits, creating someone who "displays two or more contrasting (alter) personalities that exchange control over his/her behaviour."[28] Each identity might have its own name and corresponding personality. In the 1973 book *Sybil* (later made into a TV movie starring Sally Field), the titular character had sixteen alters, including the "angry pixie" Peggy Lou, the young proto-goth named Marcia, and the redhead with a "willowy figure" named Vanessa.[29]

According to Colin Ross, his studies have found that

15% of psychiatric patients have some type of dissociative disorder, with 4% having undiagnosed DID. In the general population, he says, about 1% have some sort of DID, and that the more extreme cases, he estimates at being "1-in-500 [or] 1-in-1,000; somewhere in that kind of ballpark."[30]

These numbers, if true, are staggering. That would mean that over 3.2 million people are walking around with some form of DID. It would be more common than schizophrenia[31] and on par with bipolar disorder.[32]

If doctors like Colin Ross and groups like the ISST-D are correct, there is an epidemic of dissociation in our culture, one that has gone unrecognized by the medical community and the culture at large.

And if the conspiracy theorists are right, the epidemic has largely been caused by the CIA.

2

MK-ULTRA was the CIA cryptonym for a mind control research program initiated in 1953 by then-director Allen Dulles.[33] The idea was to find the chemical key for mind control and/or a chemical means of torture. (The euphemisms that the government used were "behavior modification" and "interrogation," respectively.) Most famously, the government funded academic LSD research through the program,[34] although many other techniques were studied. The United States has not really reckoned with this part of its history, has never held those responsible for the abuses of mind control experimentation to account. As a result, MK-ULTRA is a favorite topic of conspiracy theorists, whose claims about the program outstrip any available evidence.

Colin Ross wrote extensively about MK-ULTRA in his book *The CIA Doctors: Human Rights Violations by American Psychiatrists*. And in another one of his books, he presented evidence that the CIA mind control experiments might not be a thing of the past.

Military Mind Control is the case study of Terese, a

psychotherapist who was 30 years old when she first came to Ross for a consultation in 1992. Terese, it turns out, was in pretty bad shape—according to Ross, her father was an unstable alcoholic who abused her sexually and submitted her to Satanic ritual abuse. Ross diagnosed Terese with dissociative disorder not otherwise specified (DDNOS), "which is manifested in ego-dystonic self-mutilation and suicidal urges. She has a highly restricted social life and severe panic disorder."

In a dispassionate, clinical voice, *Military Mind Control* presents Terese's various "internally visualized ego states" (alternate personalities). These include 8-year-old Terese, "a traumatized child with no skin who lives in the back of an internal cave," and Daniella, "an introject of the outside Daniella who is sexually provocative in dress, but tasteful."

After familiarizing himself with Terese's case, Ross got down to the work of "mapping" her "internal world" through a series of interviews. Colin Ross, like many other DID therapists, is an intrepid explorer, entering into the psyche of his patient to fully sketch out "over here" parts and "over there" parts, endeavoring to achieve "clarification of the internal landscape" without activating "die commands," booby traps left by unscrupulous government hypnotists.

Recovered memory therapy has its own jargon and its own theoretical framework, resulting in long passages (the entire book, really) that read like they were translated into another language and back into English by Google:

Her internal world was mapped and subdivided into regions including: over here, over there, up above, and in between. At the back of the beginning and overlapping a bit with the back of over here and over there, was the sex world.

"The scenario was very similar to that in Richard Condon's novel *The Manchurian Candidate* and in the book by Donald Bain, *The Control of Candy Jones*," according to Ross. The latter is a classic conspiracist text that purports to be the true story of a CIA mind control victim. Tellingly, Jones's memories of mind control were unearthed using hypnosis. The hypnotist was Jones's husband "Long John" Nebel, a New York radio personality whose show featured paranormal and conspiracy topics (sort of an early Art Bell).[*]

At times, this book compares Terese's psyche to a subterranean system of tunnels and chambers; and at other times, it's presented as being a large, dysfunctional family— the various alter personalities are almost like siblings, parents, aunts, and uncles, acting up, fighting for control, often times playing dirty. The book reads like one large, 95-page mixed metaphor.

[*] According to Paul Krassner, "*The Control of Candy Jones* . . . was ghostwritten by her husband, carnival hypnotist and late-night radio talk show host 'Long John' Nebel. His friend, stage magician and psychic debunker James 'The Amazing' Randi, told me that Nebel made the entire book up because he needed the money." Krassner, *Murder at the Conspiracy Convention*, pp. 288-9

Ross's cartographic exploration of Terese's psyche was aided with psychiatric drugs. At first, Terese was on Prozac, and while this relieved some of her symptoms, it interfered with her psychotherapy, so they discontinued its use. Later on in the process, Ross conducted a drug-assisted interview with 6mg of lorazepam.

At one point, while digging around inside Terese's mind, Ross discovered "a programmed fugue state" which, if triggered, would cause her to drive to Houston and assume a new identity. But Ross, with his deft mind (de)programming abilities, claimed he could install "access codes" in his patient's mind that "could activate my or Terese's mother's phone numbers when in a safe situation, and call one of us, should such a fugue ever occur."

Ultimately, Terese's psychological problems resulted from a grotesque parody of something that many families can relate to: "By getting kicked out of" a CIA mind control program code-named Monarch, "Terese became a disappointment to her father, to whom she developed an 'unresolved ambivalent attachment.'" She was also dealing with "a core unresolved theme" that involved being judged by the Monarch mind control doctors. Terese's daddy issues and problems with authority might seem almost quaint, if it wasn't for the incest and the multiple personalities (I mean, "internally visualized ego states").

The book continues like this for a while, until it just sort of... stops.

A government mind control program called Monarch comes up quite a bit in *Military Mind Control*. Ross mentions it casually, in passing, without further explanation, as if its existence is a well-known and established fact.

> Through the end of June Terese continued to work on core themes related to getting kicked out of Monarch. This theme had been re-played relentlessly throughout her life in the form of her not fitting in and attributing this to flaws in herself, e.g., not fitting in with parents at her son's school: she doesn't even want to be friends with these people, yet she is deeply hurt by not fitting in. The core double bind/paradox is that not fitting in and getting kicked out of Monarch was a triumph and a victory—a little girl won a chess game against the Monarch program.[35]

Unlike MK-ULTRA, which is a historical certainty (even if the CIA ordered all the documents destroyed, leaving the precise contours of the program open to question), Monarch is so top secret that there is absolutely no proof it has ever existed.

Project Monarch was "discovered" when a mind control "expert," with no credentials to speak of, named Mark Phillips placed his wife Cathy O'Brien under hypnosis and began the hard work of recovering her repressed memories.[36] Among the memories hidden in her psyche was the following bombshell:

O'Brien allegedly recovered repressed memories of her training as a sex slave and drug courier for the CIA, during which time, she reports, she was sexually abused by a who's who of American public life, including President George H.W. Bush and then-first lady Hillary Clinton. O'Brien's indoctrination into a life of sexual submission allegedly began with childhood abuse by family members and Catholic priests.[37]

Another conspiracy theorist "deprogrammer," Fritz Springmeier, elaborated on Project Monarch in his newsletter, *A Newsletter from a Christian Ministry*.[38]

"The Monarch Slave's primary duty is to perpetuate the secrecy surrounding The Illuminati's Satanic activities," Springmeier reports. They are also used for "snuff films and other inhuman acts." Monarch slaves claim to communicate with extraterrestrials, but this is just a New World Order con. "This programming is part of a vast scheme to inculcate almost religious belief in aliens that will culminate in a mock alien invasion, whose real purpose is to create a ruthless One-World Government."

A cynic might say that the whole thing was invented to sell Cathy O'Brien's book, *Trance:Formation of America: The True Life Story of a CIA Mind Control Slave*.

At the time of the Project Monarch revelations in the early 1990s, the story was considered too implausible for even most conspiracy theorists. But over the years the Monarch myth has been endlessly repeated and embellished upon, and that very repetition has come to be taken as proof of the story's validity. Nowadays, people refer to Monarch as if it is, indeed, a substantiated historical fact.

In 2009, the Hollywood United Methodist Church hosted a fundraiser for the nonprofit Children of the Night, featuring appearances by "government whistleblowers" Cathy O'Brien and Mark Phillips, Colin Ross, and Roseanne Barr, who has been talking about Monarch mind control for years.

"In addition to being a champion for the rights of abused children everywhere," says a press release for the event, Roseanne "was treated by Dr. Colin Ross for DID recovery."[39]

MK-ULTRA and Monarch have become infamous among conspiracy theorists. Both terms are synonymous with government mind control, real and imagined.

"The MK-ULTRA program today is grossly misunderstood," says H.P. Albarelli Jr., the author of *A Terrible Mistake: The Murder of Frank Olson and the CIA's Secret Cold War Experiments*. According to Albarelli, what we call the CIA's MK-ULTRA mind control program wasn't a unified project as much as a disparate group of research projects under a common funding umbrella. "MK-ULTRA was simply a name that was used as a financial tracking code" for funding mind control experiments, most of which were conducted in universities. There were about 150 projects that received MK-ULTRA funds in total.

"The subcontractors really were left to their own devices, in terms of what they wanted to do," Albarelli continues. "Generally they would be told by the agency that we'd like some research done on LSD or some other drug, but the subcontractor was left to their own devices and their own objectives."

That is not to say that the MK-ULTRA mind control projects didn't have their victims.

"I'd say about 90% of them were college or university students," according to Albarelli. "And they were unwitting subjects generally in drug experiments, LSD being a fairly large part of it. But that was it. That was the program. And anybody that claims otherwise is just delusional."

The worst excesses of MK-ULTRA were bad enough that there should be no reason to embellish this history. Probably the most abusive MK-ULTRA subcontractor was Dr. Ewen Cameron. Before he died of a heart attack in 1967, the man that some call "the godfather of Canadian psychiatry"[40] had been president of the American Psychiatric Association, Canadian Psychiatric Association, American Psychopathological Association, and the Society of Biological Psychiatry. He was also the first president of the World Psychiatric Association.[41] His main area of research was finding a cure for schizophrenia.[42]

In the book *The Search for the Manchurian Candidate*, John Marks tells the story of Lauren G., one of Cameron's subjects. Married at an early age to a man she didn't love, she had a nervous breakdown in 1959. The breakdown "was a combination of my trying to lose weight, sleep loss, and my nerves," she told Marks. Ewen Cameron was supposed to be the best shrink around, so it only made sense that Lauren would be sent to Allan Memorial and placed under his care.

As it turns out, the doctor was something of an evil genius, and his treatment of Laura involved an experimental procedure of his known as "depatterning." The goal of depatterning was to wipe the mind clean, like taking an eraser to a whiteboard. The theory (and it was just a vague notion, really; there was no evidence to back this up) was that if a schizophrenic is given complete amnesia, they'll slowly regain their memories, sans the schizophrenia.

Depatterning began with ECT, or electroconvulsive therapy (shock treatments), which Marks describes as being twenty or forty times more intense than the normal therapeutic dose. The shocks would be administered two or three times a day, depending on the patient (in traditional ECT, a single shock was typically administered every one or two days). When not being shocked, the patient was kept asleep with a cocktail of Thorazine, Nembutal, Seconal, Veronal, and Phenergan.

"Sleep therapy" would generally last from 15-30 days, although sometimes patients were kept asleep and administered ECT for periods as long as 65 days. Lauren G. was one of the lucky ones—or more accurately, one of the less unlucky ones. She "gradually recovered full recall of her life before the treatment," writes Marks. With other patients, the ECT was more severe, and LSD or PCP were added to the chemical cocktail.

After the mind was blanked out by depatterning, the victims were subjected to "psychic driving." This involved forcing the subject to listen to recorded messages on a loop, for 16-hours at a time. The messages were meant to eradicate negative behavior and reinforce positive behavior.

Cameron was clearly a madman well before he first received MK-ULTRA funding in 1957. As the grants came through a CIA front organization called the Society for the Investigation of Human Ecology, there has been some question as to whether Cameron was aware of CIA involvement in his program at all. Not that it matters much —the fact that the CIA had even heard about his experiments and decided that they wanted to jump into bed with him says a lot about the agency, and a lot about MK-ULTRA.

Between 1957 and 1961, Cameron performed his experiments on 53 people.[43] He received more than $60,000 from the CIA for the program, while the Canadian government gave him around $200,000 for this research. All told, the number of victims of Cameron's "psychic driving" experiments is around 80.[44] In 1992, the Canadian government said it would pay his victims $80,000 each in compensation. And since then, the government of Canada has continued to settle lawsuits related to the experimentation.[45]

3

When we met in the lobby of the Palmer House in Chicago, Colin Ross was easily recognizable from his pictures on the internet. After being introduced to his wife and daughter, I followed Ross to the conference area above the hotel lobby. I smiled and nodded mutely as he asked some people with the ISST-D if we could use a room for our interview. After a round of hugs between Ross and the staffers, we were led to a private room. We spent the next hour discussing dissociative identity disorder, CIA mind control conspiracy theories, and the points where those two topics intersect. The one thing I really wanted to know was: How does a Manchurian Candidate end up in the office of Dr. Ross?

"If someone comes into civilian therapy," Ross said, "there's two lines of thinking on that. One is, we see the people who've blown a fuse, they're defective, they don't any longer have utility. That's going to make the military establishment a little antsy, right?" According to Ross, this might be the real purpose of groups like the False Memory Syndrome Foundation—to put a lid on the legitimate claims of government mind control victims.

"That's obviously a good strategy for shutting the whole thing down and discrediting" recovered memory therapy, he said.

But it could be that the mind control victims he sees in his practice aren't malfunctioning at all.

"Sometimes it's actually an [intelligence] operation," he continued. "They're sending their Manchurian Candidate to you, just to see if you can deprogram them. Then that person goes back and reports back to their handler, and this is what she said, and this is what she's doing. Because they want expertise on counter-intelligence use of all this technology, so that they can detect and dismantle Manchurian Candidates being run at them."

Ross admitted, however, that these are just theories. "That's all just conjecture," he says. "Who's got facts?"

We spoke for a while longer, touching on Naziism, the Harvey Weinstein scandal, and the John Travolta film *The General's Daughter* before I felt like I'd had enough. I wasn't entirely sure what I got out of our conversation, but I was convinced that if we talked for another two hours, it wouldn't help me any.

As I mentioned earlier, in addition to wanting an interview with Ross, I figured that a past president of the ISST-D should be able to throw his weight around a bit and get me into the conference for free. As we were saying our goodbyes, I asked him if this would be possible. He countered by suggesting that I purchase a day pass for $379.

"I'd really like to see your presentation, to include it in

my story," I told him. "Maybe I could just go in with you, and trail you for the afternoon."

"That's not how this is going to play out," he said, which seemed like a really awkward turn of phrase.

If Ross couldn't (didn't want to) swing a press pass for yours truly, I decided to cross over to the dark side—specifically, I got a ride across town to Wicker Park to watch The Satanic Temple at work.

"You're going to my favorite neighborhood," the Lyft driver told me.

"Which neighborhood is that?" I asked.

"I call it 'hipster paradise.'"

I told him to take me there anyway.

At a video production studio, I was greeted by a Satanist named Sarah Ponto Rivera. After introducing me to some of her fellow Templars, she exited the room to apply her on-camera makeup. The group, as a whole, were very friendly, all very serious about exposing the dark underbelly of the ISST-D. There was one point when I started to sneeze, and as I started to sneeze, the thought occurred to me: what *does* a Satanist say when somebody sneezes?

Then I sneezed.

"Bless you," said one of my hosts, immediately and without thinking. Nobody else in the room noticed, so I appreciated the irony in silence.[*]

---

[*] There are also Satanists out there who say "curse you" when you

The co-founder of The Satanic Temple arrived a few minutes after I did. Now, *this* guy looks like a Satanist, I thought. He was dressed in black, and his eyes were different colors, sort of like David Bowie. When he wasn't working to change society, he wouldn't look out of place at an industrial music night somewhere.

Lucien Greaves (née Doug Messner) co-founded The Satanic Temple in 2012 and acts as its spokesperson.[46] To paraphrase the Discordians (a parody religion of the 1960s), The Satanic Temple appears to be either an elaborate publicity stunt disguised as a serious religion, or a serious religion disguised as an elaborate publicity stunt. Temple chapters across the country have taken part in a number of actions that don't seem at all evil or scary in the least, including protests in support of Planned Parenthood[47] and pledging support for the American Muslim community after the Paris terror attacks in 2015.[48] Most recently, the group erected a bronze statue of Baphomet alongside the Ten Commandments monument at the Arkansas State Capitol building, to protest for the separation of church and state.[49]

According to Greaves, there are 100,000 people around the world who count themselves as members of his organization.

It must be said before we go any further that The Satanic Temple are not "devil worshippers," in the *Necronomicon*-backmasking-*Dungeons & Dragons*-high

sneeze, and "go to Heaven" when you piss them off.

school stoner sense. The group, more than anything, is post-Christian.

"The Satan of Milton resonates for us, the ultimate rebel against tyranny," Greaves told me. "We view Satan and Satanism as kind of the metaphorical, mythological backdrop for enlightenment values, rather than those kind of authoritarian, medieval values" embraced by Christendom.

The Satanic Temple's view on the ISST-D is straightforward: to the extent that dissociative identity disorder (DID) exists, it is iatrogenic—caused by the treating doctor through bad and discredited therapeutic practices. But if DID is pseudoscience and the doctors treating it dangerous, the ISST-D is instrumental in giving these doctors a sort of "respectable" veneer.

After Sarah was made up, and Lucien grudgingly assented to the use of a little powder or something so that his skin wouldn't reflect so much under the studio lighting, they took their places in front of the camera to record a video to release to the media on the heels of Saturday's protest.

When I began this investigation, I endeavored to refer to the condition where a person is believed to possess multiple personalities as dissociative identity disorder (DID), because that's the current, accepted nomenclature.

I don't think I'm going to be able to do that going forward.

I guess that I lied. I mean, I *tried*. I was a good sport about the whole thing, but "dissociative identity disorder" is such a mouthful. And it gives the wrong impression. It's a whitewash, really, a semantic cover-up by those who wish to avoid the surreal nature of what is going on in these patients. The term "multiple personality disorder" is much more satisfying artistically, much more evocative, and probably more clinically accurate as well. So, for now on that's what we'll be discussing; not DID, but MPD.

Before his untimely death in a single-engine plane crash in 1994, Nicholas P. Spanos was a Professor of Psychology and Director of the Laboratory for Experimental Hypnosis at Carleton University in Ottawa.[50] In his landmark book *Multiple Identities & False Memories: A Sociocognitive Perspective*, Spanos looks at the nature of multiple personality disorder and makes the point that the specific shape of MPD has been determined by our culture. If MPD didn't exist in its current form until quite recently, it's because whatever impulses underlay MPD found different forms of expression in the past.

"Toward the end of the 19th century," Spanos writes, "multiple personality was considered a species of hysteria and had become an established and, at least in France and in America, a relatively common disorder." Common, yes, but not the same as what we call MPD nowadays. As noted by pioneering French psychiatrist Pierre Janet (1859-1947), investigators "who diagnosed and treated MPD patients with relative frequency, did not regularly discover child sexual abuse as a cause of their patients' symptoms." These days, however, MPD is almost always (if not always) thought to be the product of childhood sexual abuse.

"Modern investigators who frequently diagnose MPD have borrowed Janet's use of leading hypnotic interviews and age-regression procedures to diagnose and treat MPD," Spanos continues. And in doing so, they seem to have recreated MPD in their own image, resulting in "a modern 'epidemic' of MPD patients whose alters are often first discovered during hypnotic therapy and whose 'dissociative splits' are usually traced to memories of childhood sexual abuse that emerged during such therapy."[51]

I bring all this up at this point in the narrative because understanding why MPD is controversial in the first place is key to understanding why the Satanists find the ISST-D so objectionable. To The Satanic Temple, MPD is clearly pseudoscience, an accident of poor therapeutic technique. And since it is often the case that, among the ISST-D, mythical "Satanists" get the blame for causing multiple personality disorder, The Satanic Temple takes this issue very seriously.

The next night, I was back in Northwest Chicago, at a community art space where The Satanic Temple was rehearsing a street theater protest piece. As a phalanx of Satanists stood in the back of the room, holding signs with slogans like: "BURN Pseudoscience NOT Witches" and "ISSTD INFANTILIZES WOMEN," a man in a blazer with "ISSTD" painted on the back coaxed a long scarf into a young woman's mouth; she's dressed like one of the inmates in the video for "Psycho Therapy" by the Ramones. At the conclusion of the spectacle, the scarf was removed from her mouth and held up in the air, revealing the message "PSEUDOSCIENCE KILLS." As all of this is going on, yet another Satanist reads a manifesto of sorts:

> [N]o longer will we stand idle as mental health professionals continue to denigrate their patients. No longer will we be silent as women are infantilized under the cloak of trauma therapy. No longer will we watch as reports of documented sexual abuse go ignored by the ISSTD while they instill false memories of the abuse they want to hear.

At the conclusion of the speech, she brought it all home with the slogan: "Protect the victims of the ISSTD. *Fuck pseudoscience.*"

After several run-throughs, the Satanists were content that all the rough edges had been smoothed out, and I was briefed on the plan for Saturday. I was told to be in the hotel lobby before noon. When the ISST-D broke for lunch, the Satanists would appear, marching through the conference space, into the lobby, and out the door. Once outside, the guerrilla theater piece they'd been rehearsing would commence.

The next morning, I got to the bar in the lobby with fifteen minutes to kill. People were eating mostly, some were drinking beer, and a few sightseers were using their phones to take pictures of Louis Pierre Rigal's frescoes on the ceiling above.[52]

I ordered a Miller High Life and waited.

After my second beer, I realized something was wrong. I shouldn't even have had time to finish the one beer before the action kicked off; so I walked outside to see what exactly was going on. The Satanist theater troupe was nowhere to be found, while Lucien and Sarah were on the sidewalk, conferring with a couple other people from their organization. A documentary filmmaker who was in town to film the Temple wandered off to buy a cookie at a nearby bakery, and a man with an enormous pot-bellied pig on a leash handed out flyers protesting the ISST-D in front of the CVS across the street.

I learned that hotel security had caught the Satanists and ejected them from the hotel through an out-of-the-way exit, temporarily short-circuiting the planned action. The group eventually reconvened on the sidewalk near the entrance to the hotel and commenced the performance without any further hindrance.

When I think of Chicago cops, I usually think of the riot during the 1968 Democratic convention. When law enforcement arrived on the scene of the 2018 ISST-D protest, the vibe was much different than I was expecting. The police were altogether nonplussed by the Satanists. And the cop cars were white with a dash of cyan blue, which was both non-threatening and redolent of a tube of gel toothpaste.

"Compared to the other protest, this isn't any trouble at

all," one cop said, referring to the thousands of angry young people who had descended on Union Park two miles west, in response to the Parkland high school massacre.

Aside from the police, the only other real audience for the guerrilla theater action was a group of guys in matching blue windbreakers. One was holding a sign advertising AT&T wireless service.

"I'm hella confused," a young man with an afro yelled as the Satanists wound down their performance, causing his friends to break into laughter.

At first, I wondered if the Satanists were discouraged by the size of the audience that their action drew. Then I realized that while the protest might have taken place on a city sidewalk, it was meant for YouTube. It was merely the latest salvo in a sustained campaign against recovered memory therapy. And that every protest action by The Satanic Temple is one more blow that the ISST-D has to absorb. It only remains to be seen how much fight the ISST-D has left.

4

Unwilling to hand over the steep conference fee, I was truly annoyed that I couldn't get in to see the conference for myself. I hung out at the bar in the lobby every night, trying to meet some members of the ISST-D, with little luck. Finally, on my last night in Chicago, I met a whistleblower of sorts—a mental health professional who was willing to share what he saw over the course of the weekend. I promised to keep his identity a secret, so let's just call him *Fabio*.

One thing I wondered was, did the ISST-D keep its craziness under wraps? Or were people actually airing their most outrageous claims—Satanic Ritual Abuse, CIA mind control, that sort of thing—in the presentations?

"Well," Fabio said, "they're trying to keep a lid on it. They're trying to keep a lid on what they really believe, and they've actually been doing that for a long time." But if normality was the goal, the group didn't really do a very good job at it.

One example of the ISST-D weirdness occurred when Fabio arrived early for a presentation with the title: "The

Migration Model: A New Approach to Mind Control Treatment in Ritual Abuse Clients." The presenter was Eileen Aveni, a shrink in Ann Arbor and a past chair of the ISST-D's Ritual Abuse/Mind Control/Organized Abuse special interest group. It's safe to say that her beliefs weren't terribly far afield from what the ISST-D believes as a whole.

"I walked into the room too early," Fabio said. "There was only one other person in there, and she immediately started asking me questions, you know. Where was I from, what kind of work did I do?" Not the sort of attention you want to have when you're trying to lay low and whistleblow. "She wanted to know, do you have a lot of RA clients? And I didn't catch it, 'ritual abuse,' right away. I'm used to the old language, SRA—'Satanic ritual abuse.' I said, 'RA?' And then she was immediately suspicious of me."

After the other attendees arrived, Aveni began her presentation. Fabio called it "the most fantastic, just pulled-out-of-her-ass therapeutic approach with mind control and ritual abuse clients you ever fucking heard." Aveni is running an experimental therapeutic technique that posits that her patients "have these incredibly elaborate internal systems," Fabio explained. What he described sounds a lot like Colin Ross's work with the military mind control victim he called Terese. "It's like a *Dungeons and Dragons* or a video game world, with tunnels and private rooms and ... control panels and switches and different stages of leaders and protectors."

The crowd might've been confused, but at least one

person present was truly moved by Eileen Aveni's story: Eileen Aveni herself.

"It's just literally taking her breath away," Fabio said. Aveni's story "brings her to tears" in front of her audience.

Fabio, who received continuing education credits from the American Psychological Association for attending the conference (it's frightening to think of how many mental health therapists might be "trained" in such nonsense every year), said that most of the speakers he saw that weekend "were much more skilled at appearing to be semi-reasonable, and they did not go into a lot of floridly wacky stuff."

As for his fellow conference attendees, "they seemed like kind of a rickety bunch to me," Fabio said. "This is going to sound terrible, but [they were] physically and mentally a little wobbly. Some of them weren't, some of the younger people. But there were mostly older people there. That's why I kind of had mixed feelings about all of this, because obviously it wasn't a lot of people there, maybe 300, and a lot of them seemed as though kind of probably not top-of-the-line in their fields."

This hasn't been the easiest story to report, because the ISST-D crowd obfuscates its more outré beliefs with clinical and "scientistic" language. But a couple of times throughout the week, I've been presented with an image that cuts through all that bullshit.

"One of the most striking moments I had in the entire conference," according to Fabio, was at the Saturday night awards dinner. "They're getting into the awards, and all of a sudden on the screen appears the Cornelia B. Wilbur award."

We both laughed. Cornelia Wilbur was the psychiatrist who wrote the book *Sybil*. This is the story Shirley Mason (called Sybil in the book). Born and raised in Minnesota, Mason moved to New York City in 1953 to attend graduate school at Columbia Teachers College.

Things were not going well for Mason when she sought out therapy. She was experiencing a number of disturbing symptoms, including fatigue, depression, and pain throughout the body. Soon after her treatment with Wilbur began, Shirley Mason found herself prescribed "powerful, habit-forming drugs," according to Debbie Nathan, author of *Sybil Exposed*, "many of which had just been patented in the 1950s and were being aggressively marketed by pharmaceutical companies." These drugs included Seconal, whose withdrawal symptoms include anxiety, strange dreams, and hallucinations; Demerol, an opiate whose side-effects can include blackouts; and two painkillers, Edrisal and Daprisal, that combined aspirin with amphetamine.

"Edrisal and Daprisal eventually proved so addictive that they were yanked from the market," Nathan writes. "Soon Shirley was in her second semester at Teachers College, still managing to attend classes and complete her school work. But she spent her free time half zonked on mind-bending medications."

Wilbur diagnosed Mason as having dissociative fugue states. And not long after that, Mason was coming to her therapy sessions as different characters, with names like

Peggy and Vicky. If Wilbur had known that Vicky was Mason's childhood imaginary friend, and that Peggy was a character from one of her childhood games, she might have considered that her patient was devising ways to keep her attention. But she did not, and soon Wilbur came to believe that Shirley Mason had four alter personalities—nothing too impressive these days, when an MPD sufferer will claim to have dozens if not hundreds of alters, but a huge number for the 1950s. Eventually, Wilbur had Mason strung out on sodium amytal; the number of Shirley Mason's alters increased to ten, then sixteen.

At one point, Mason admitted to her therapist that the fugue states and the alters were lies concocted to keep Wilbur's interest. The two had become enmeshed in a grotesque of the doctor-patient dynamic, and Mason, at least, felt guilty about it.

"I am not going to tell you there isn't anything wrong [with me]," Mason wrote in a letter to her therapist in 1956. "But it is not what I have led you to believe. . . I do not have any multiple personalities. . . I do not even have a 'double.'"

And, later, in that same letter: "I am all of them. I have been essentially lying."[53]

In 1977, the journalist Flora Rheta Schreiber published the book *Sybil*, which told Mason's story, written with Mason and Wilbur's assistance. At the time of its publication, *Sybil* solidified Wilbur's reputation as a pioneering psychiatrist.

It's hard to believe that the ISST-D would be so dense

as to hand out an award that's named after Cornelia B. Wilbur, so many years after she'd been discredited. But it makes sense once you realize that the ISST-D exists in an alternate reality, one where the CIA is churning out Manchurian candidates to use for mind control sex slaves.

The ISST-D is "gathered in a room," Fabio said, expressing the absurdity of the whole scene. "Ostensibly they're facing down an international cult of very skilled torturers and murderers, and they have a painting party in the evening, and they're tittering over a little joke somebody had made. And they're happy to see each other. If you really believed that shit, would you go anywhere near the Palmer House?"

It's no surprise that Fabio came out of the experience seeing the ISST-D as being, on the whole, a very dysfunctional group.

"I don't think anybody's making a lot of money," Fabio says. "I think it's got more to do with the type of person. Like a real sort of flawed, Messiah-complex individual, whose main benefit from all this is their sense of heroism. It's not as simple as 'do they believe this or not?'"

Ultimately, it looks like the ISST-D is quasi-fundamentalist, quasi-religious. Either you believe its oddball theories, and you're on the inside, or you don't, and you're forever on the outside. And if you're on the outside, you probably won't have any idea of what's really going on with the organization.

"It's a cult!" Fabio exclaims. "This *is* the cult. Their motto should be 'we are the people we've been fighting.'"

We both get a good laugh out of this. It reminds me of the old Walt Kelly *Pogo* cartoon: "We have met the enemy and he is us."

5

By the time I returned home from Chicago, I had read far too many of Colin Ross's books. In addition to *Military Mind Control* and *The CIA Doctors*, there was a satirical treatise called *The Great Psychiatry Scam: One Shrink's Personal Journey*, in which he critiques his profession. There is also *The Osiris Complex: Case Studies in Multiple Personality Disorder*, in which Ross relates a number of cases every bit as bizarre as that of Terese, the Monarch mind control victim from his book *Military Mind Control*.

In a chapter titled "Flash and the Destroyer," Ross talks about a woman named Margaret, "a thin, pale woman in her early twenties, with straight brown hair and a fearful, pinched, withdrawn manner." Her history, he says, was vague ("there were many large amnesiac gaps in her life") but between the anxiety, depression, the substance abuse and the dissociation, she was a good candidate for an MPD diagnosis. And sure enough, as soon as Ross sits down with Margaret he is able to summon Margaret's "inner child"—literally, an alter that identified itself as "Maggie," age 5.

Ross agrees to work with the young woman, and claims that "Within several months, Margaret provided me a map of a complex personality system which was highly structured and detailed."

> It consisted of two "communities," each arranged in a circle, with two small circles joining the two larger circles. Within each of the two communities, there were three sets of alters Margaret called "families," and within each family there were three sets of paired alters she called "sisters." The families were arranged in concentric circles within the communities.
>
> The two smaller circles in-between the two larger circles were observed personalities overlooking each community, one called Guide and one called Observer. "Observer" is one of the names frequently met in MPD personality systems, and "Guide" is also fairly common. These two entities held a record of all the life experience of all the alters in their respective communities, and also communicated with each other. At the beginning of therapy, however, the two communities were completely amnesiac for each other.

After mapping her "personality system" and meeting several of Margaret's alters, Ross makes the acquaintance of Violet, an alter who was used to film child porn. Since

Pine-Sol cleaning product was used to clean the movie set, Margaret (and Violet) "developed a post-traumatic, hyperaroused reaction to Pinesol [sic], without knowing why."

Eventually, Margaret recovers memories of being used by extraterrestrial entities to produce hybrid human-alien offspring. "If the abductions are real," Ross helpfully points out, "it would appear that the human race is being used as breeders, with amnesia for the human participation implanted hypnotically by the aliens."

It was while working with Margaret that Ross realized there is some sort of connection between UFO abductions and Satanic ritual abuse.

"In thinking about what was real in Margaret's stories, and what fantasy," he writes, "it was not easy to determine where to draw the line. I don't want to make the kind of mistake 'good Germans' did who looked the other way and pretended Auschwitz didn't exist, if there is a Satanic Third Reich active in North America today. On the other hand, I don't want to be the dupe of mass hysteria and urban legend."

Probably the most serious incident during Margaret's treatment occurs when she slips into a "catatonic coma" for three days.

"Margaret was the kind of patient who, in the nineteenth century, was called a grand hysteric," Ross writes. "Her dissociative performances were virtuoso."

Margaret eventually wakes up, after which she discontinued her treatment. Ever the humble healer, Ross eventually concluded that some people just can't be helped. Not even by Colin Ross.

"Margaret taught me that I am unable to treat everyone with MPD," he concludes. "Perhaps the next revolution in psychiatry will provide a conceptual framework and therapy techniques which can help people like Margaret more effectively than the classical MPD psychotherapy of the late twentieth century. I hope so."

In *The Osiris Complex*, Ross gives us a front row seat to the inner workings of recovered memory therapy. It all seems impossible; probably because it is impossible. As University of California, Irvine memory researcher Elizabeth F. Loftus explained to me recently, memory just doesn't work the way that people like Ross and members of the ISST-D claim. Recovered memories, she said, are actually new memories that are suggested by therapists.

Typically, according to Loftus, someone goes to a therapist with a pretty standard complaint—depression, anxiety, or an eating disorder—and the therapist says this complaint isn't *really* the problem, that it's actually a symptom of past abuse buried in the patient's memory.

"Even when the patient denies it," Loftus says, "the therapist might give a little education about repressed memories or start to use techniques like guided imagery," things that can be used to implant memories in impressionable patients.

Loftus and her colleagues have studied the techniques of

repressed memory therapy, and they've learned to implant memories of things that have never happened. Of course, this doesn't mean that repressed memories don't exist—only that false memories can be created in an experimental setting. So I ask her, *is* there any evidence for repressed memories?

"Well," she says, "when you look at what the repression aficionados put forward as their proof of repressed memory, it's not proof at all."

Possibly the most important study supporting claims of repression is a 1994 study by the sociologist Linda Meyer Williams. In "Recall of Childhood Trauma: A Prospective Study of Women's Memories of Child Sexual Abuse," Williams tracked down 129 women who had been to a hospital emergency room in a major northeastern city, all victims of sexual abuse. All they were told was that they were selected because they'd been seen in the hospital as a child; sexual abuse was never mentioned. Williams found that thirty-eight percent of the people she interviewed about their medical history didn't mention the abuse. This she interpreted to mean that thirty-eight percent of the people in her study repressed their abuse memories.[54]

"You know," Loftus says, "here are some people who were under the age of 12 in the 1970s, and now somebody comes back to them an average of 17 years later," and interviews them about their life. "They're mostly in their 20s or 30s, you talk to them for two hours. And they don't mention the abuse."*

Yeah, I say. I can imagine a lot of people wouldn't mention their childhood abuse to a complete stranger.

"Exactly. Well, thirty-eight percent did not mention it."

In *Memory Warp: How the Myth of Repressed Memory Arose and Refuses to Die*, science writer Mark Pendergrast offers a number of alternate explanations for Williams' findings. Probably the most interesting thing about the study is that 68 percent of those who didn't specifically cite the incident that caused them to go to the hospital in the first place did report other incidents of sexual abuse. "It seems safe to assume that anyone who was *routinely* subjected to abuse might not remember every single time it occurred," he writes. "In other words, we may not be dealing with 'repression' so much as a particular incident lost in a flood of repeated abuse." Or someone might not have reported the incident because they felt it "may not have been traumatic enough to report in the context of this particular interview." They may have recalled the abuse and not wanted to talk about it. Or they might have forgotten about it. "We do not remember everything— even every bad thing— that has ever happened to us. It is not necessary to assume that such forgetting involves psychological defense mechanisms" like repression.[55]

Repressed and recovered memories are almost always the sole proof of abuse that a ritual abuse victim has. But if

* Loftus misspoke; the interviews were actually an average of three hours. Still, the point stands.

memories can't really be repressed and recovered, that means the "proof" of abuse isn't proof at all. There must be some sort of motivation for a person to believe that horrifying, unprovable things happened in their past.

"They got a problem," Loftus says. "They've either got their symptoms, or they're not accomplishing as much in life as they would've wanted to, or they're in trouble with the law or other ways—substance abuse—and they now have an explanation. You don't want to be crazy. You don't want to be a bad person. So, you know, the more palatable explanation is that 'I was abused.'"

In other words, someone goes into therapy looking for a strategy to cope with their unmanageable life, and the trauma therapist gives them one. Sure, it's a strategy that can involve extraterrestrials, Satanic cults, and strange powers of the mind, but all that proves is that, under the right conditions, people can be persuaded to believe the most improbable, fantastical things.

6

In October 1986, Roma Hart was a single parent, a student at the University of Manitoba, and had recently lost her job at a Holiday Inn hotel. She had been receiving unemployment insurance, but it was set to run out. Then a friend told her that she could get her benefits extended due to stress, as long as a doctor signed off on it.

"So I took the form over and I met the student counselor" at the University of Manitoba, she told me over the phone. Her unemployment insurance was set to run out, "but I'm a university student, I'm a single mom—that qualifies as being under stress, don't you think?"

In response, the student counselor asked what Hart did when she was stressed out.

"I'm so busy, I just switch to 'autopilot,'" Roma said. Meaning that she just sort of buckled down and did what she needed to do. But to the counselor, "autopilot" had a more ominous meaning.

"Her eyes got real big," Roma said, "and she asked me, 'do you have a name for this autopilot?'"

Roma laughed at the thought that such an innocent

remark could be taken to mean that had multiple personality disorder.

"She decided that [the autopilot] was another personality," according to Roma. "She said that her professor at the University of Manitoba was a specialist. The only specialist on multiple personality in Western Canada, and she had always wanted to work with him."

This, Roma said, is how she was introduced to Colin Ross. "And within fifteen minutes, he diagnosed me with multiple personality disorder."

In Hart's mind, this was supposed to be a harmless little scam. She would meet with the doctor and pretend to have multiple personalities and, in return, she'd receive her unemployment checks.

"I'm a theater student, by the way," she said. "I can pull this off! I had no idea that by the end of the month, I would be actually insane, and within two months I would be committed to a psych ward and forcibly injected with drugs. I had no idea my life was going to be totally ruined so fast, you know. Because I went in there totally sane, knowing what I was doing."

One of the first things that Ross did, according to Hart, was give her a checklist with "symptoms" of sexual abuse. The list was all-encompassing, the items on the list quite vague. "It doesn't matter what your symptoms are, all of your symptoms are symptoms of someone who's been sexually abused," according to Roma.

And in fact, Hart had been sexually assaulted once, by a stranger, when she was 9 years old. This disclosure only prompted Ross to insist that there must have been more instances of abuse in her past; incidents that she had repressed.

"Because my father was in the military," Hart told me, Ross suspected that she had been subjected to military mind control. Her father "was in the Air Force, he was an aerial cartographer with intelligence," and he was a Freemason. "I was like a sitting duck then, because anything to do with the military is the culture of mind control. It's where they take the children and put goggles over their eyes and they mind control you because they're going to use you later in life. So my father's in the military, he was a Mason, and oh my goodness, that's Satanism! He is part of a Satanic cult."

When Ross found out that Roma's boyfriend worked for CSIS (the Canadian Security Intelligence Service; basically, the Canadian CIA), he must have been ecstatic— he had finally found a real-life mind control victim and her handler.

"He said, 'You are one of those children that was put into mind control experiments through the military,'" Hart told me. "'You are either a gamma, a beta, or an alpha.' And I didn't know what the hell he was talking about. One was that you were programmed to commit suicide, one that you're programmed for assassination, and one you're programmed to give disinformation. And I just picked the one that sounded the least idiotic. I think I told him I was a gamma or something, only because that sounded the least idiotic to me, and I thought that was the end of it."

In *Mother Night*, Vonnegut cautions that "we must be

careful about what we pretend to be," because in the end,
we *are* who we pretend to be. Maybe Roma Hart could
have used that advice; or maybe she shouldn't have had to.

"He just made me feel less and less secure of my sanity,"
she said. "And he kept on throwing his authority around."

Just as Ross has documented in his book *The Osiris
Complex*, Roma said that he used hypnosis in their sessions.
I asked her to describe this to me.

"He would make you very relaxed," she said, "and then
he'd want to talk to [various] personalities. And you would
want to please this guy, because he was hell-bent on getting
his way, and if you resisted he would just get more
determined."

She played along.

"Then he started stroking your arms, and stroking your
legs, and..." Roma sort of trailed off, laughing nervously. "It
was a bunch of women, and he was a handsome guy, you
know, when he was young. And you just wanted to please
this guy."

Once she was in a relaxed, suggestible state, Ross would
start asking her various 'personalities' to present themselves.

"He'd say, 'Who are you?'" And Roma would give him
whatever name came to mind, picking something at
random. "He would say, 'I want to talk to this personality,
and ask questions.' So you just want to cooperate, you just
want to please this guy, you want to do anything to make
him happy."

It wasn't just Roma, either. At the time of her work
with Ross, she said that she was part of an MPD support

group at the hospital.

"We all just went along," Roma said. "It was so hard to keep these things straight! It was so hard to keep them straight. The more you'd see him, the more personalities [you had], and each personality was supposed to only remember one little bit. And we would all make the same mistakes, we'd screw up, and we'd use the wrong name, remember the wrong thing. And he'd say 'How'd you know that?' [laughs] And he'd say, 'Oh, you're Observer,' or 'You're Guide.' Everyone has an Observer or a Guide who knows everything. And that is the personality for when we fuck up, or we remember something that we're not supposed to remember. It's so stupid, but that's what Colin Ross says. Sure. You can't argue with him, it's impossible to argue with that guy."

But this was more than play-acting. Between the hypnosis and the heavy doses of Halcion (a highly-addictive benzodiazepine used to treat insomnia)[56] that she was prescribed, Roma started having 'flashbacks,' strange fantasies that Ross told her were memories that had been trapped in her subconscious.

"When I was on drugs, when I was heavily drugged, it was much easier to make me believe anything," she said.

In addition to drugs and hypnosis, Roma said that her treatment included guided meditation—which, in her drugged and highly suggestible state, further blurred the lines between fantasy and reality.

Ross would ask her if she had any memories of sexual abuse or being involved in occult rituals. "Were you ever in a ring of people wearing hoods?" Roma said. "And things like this, right? With chanting."

She would deny that anything like that had occurred in her past, but when she went home the images would be in the forefront of her consciousness.

"I'd say no, I don't remember that at all! But I'd go home and I'd think about it. And I'd go to bed, he had me listening to a tape, he made a tape for me to listen to. I'd walk around campus with it all day long, listening to it, this hypnotic tape, with suggestions. Suggestions of things that he wanted me to remember. And I'd listen to it all day long on campus, and at night time I was listening to it before I went to sleep."

At this point, Roma is describing what infamous MK-ULTRA doctor Ewen Cameron called "psychic driving," or at least a variation of it. She would then have nightmares prompted by the hypnosis tape.

"Those aren't nightmares," Roma was told. "Those are flashbacks of real memories."

According to Roma, she was under Ross's care for about five years total. The last time she saw him was in 1991. She had lost custody of her daughter after she was diagnosed with multiple personality disorder, and she realized that she would never get her daughter back as long as she was under Ross's care.

"Colin Ross told the social workers that she was in danger," Roma said. "This 9-year-old girl, sweet little angel of a girl, was in danger because of a child-murdering Satanic cult family. So she was hidden away from her whole entire family."

Eventually, Roma confronted Ross. "I said, I'm trying to get custody of my daughter, and it's not helping that I'm seeing you for MPD treatments and being on all these drugs and that. And he agreed! He was so annoyed with me anyways, 'cause I made so much trouble for him."

When she finally broke with Ross, Roma said she went to his office to ask for her journals, which he kept in the bottom drawer of his filing cabinet. It wouldn't be until later, when she unsuccessfully tried to sue Ross (the case was thrown out after it had dragged on beyond the statute of limitations) that Roma would learn that he held back some of the journals for himself. Roma's experiences would become the basis for "Margaret" from *The Osiris Complex*.

"The only way I knew this chapter was about me was because he lifted words right out of my journals several times," Roma told me in an email. "Until [my lawyer] took it out and started reading Chapter 14 during Colin Ross's first deposition I had no idea he was including my case in a book."

At one of their first therapy sessions, Roma claimed that Ross told her she had a half-alien child, somewhere in the universe. "I was a Pentecostal Christian fundamentalist" at that time, Roma said. "You don't tell that to a Pentecostal Christian fundamentalist, because the first thing that you think about is, how could God have let that happen? And what about the soul of the baby? Things like that, right? I couldn't deal with it, I couldn't talk about it." It was too upsetting to contemplate.

She "was mortified when I raised the possibility that the aliens were not literally real," Ross writes in *The Osiris Complex*.[57] "She cried profusely, and said I had ruined the therapy and her chances of recovery forever by doubting that."

Roma's version of the incident is even stranger. In 1990, after attending a conference in Chicago, she said that Ross came to her with "good news."

"Your baby didn't die," he told Roma. "[MPD psychiatrist] Bennett Braun and I, we have discovered that all the babies that have been murdered at these Satanic rituals never died. No, they'd been beamed aboard spaceships. And after they're 18, they're beamed back down to Earth and given jobs at the CIA, to form a New World Order.'"

Not only does this explain why the New World Order is so demonic, it also explains why years of Satanic ritual abuse conspiracy theories have never been able to produce any physical evidence.

"I burst into tears," Roma said. "I was quite satisfied that my baby had died and I didn't think about it anymore. No. Now he's telling me my child is alive and given a job with the CIA and the New World Order. And he couldn't figure out why I was upset!"

Probably the most upsetting part of Roma's story is that Colin Ross himself might not even believe any of this.

"I remember this so vividly," Roma said. She's telling me about her last meeting with Ross. "It's one of those weird things—you remember the weird things in your life really vividly. I asked him, why did you make me believe all those crazy stories about Satanic cults and murderers and aliens? Why did you make me believe all that?"

Ross "looked at me with this grin," Roma said, "like an Elvis Presley grin, and he said to me: 'I never believed any of that crap.' He thought it was funny."

7

On February 6, 2010, a former pharmaceutical president named Gigi Jordan was arrested and sent to Bellevue Hospital for the murder of her 8-year-old-son, Jude Mirra.[58] The boy was autistic, and the mother deeply troubled. According to Jordan, it was a "mercy killing."[59] She believed that her child had multiple personality disorder, that this was the result of a child abuse conspiracy, and that only in death would Jordan escape his tormentors.

The journey culminating in her son's death had taken them across the country over the course of several years.

On April Fool's Day in 2008, this journey found Jordan and her 6-year-old son Jude in Cheyenne, Wyoming in what is known as a "shelter care hearing." The purpose of the proceeding was to decide whether or not Jordan was fit to have custody of her son. She came to Wyoming after contacting the state's Division of Criminal Investigation (DCI), which she had discovered while researching child abuse on the internet. After several telephone calls, she surprised agents of the DCI by flying in from California unannounced.

An agent named Bruce Dexter met Jordan and her son at the airport. As he testified at the custody hearing, when she arrived in Wyoming, Jordan was "very excited." According to Dexter, he "couldn't make sense of what she was saying. She was jumping around to different topics, different areas. It was a very convoluted story."

In the following excerpts from the hearing transcript, Dexter is questioned by Assistant District Attorney Meri Ramsey:

> Q. Did you have any concerns about her [Jordan] at that time?
>
> A. Personally, I was worried she wasn't feeling well, for whatever reason. I thought there might have been some medical or [mental] health issues there. I wasn't really sure.
>
> Q: Who did she say is involved in the sexual abuse of this child?
>
> A: The initial component of this, if my recollection holds correctly, was a housekeeper -- a caretaker of this young man, a female, and it has expanded to potentially her ex-husband was implicated in this.
>
> There is also possibly a business person that she had a business arrangement with. These are certainly socially and economically, politically kind of high-

connected people.

As Wyoming authorities interacted with Jordan, they unearthed more clues that there might be something wrong with her. She had ditched her cellphone in California and refused to use her credit cards because she thought that her son's tormentors would use these items to track her movements. And among her luggage, there was no clothing for her six-year-old son. In fact, when Jude was taken into custody, he wasn't wearing socks or underwear.

Eventually, Jude Mirra received a medical examination, and despite his mother's claims that he "had been sexually assaulted and brutally sodomized, and some very terrible things had been done to him sexually by a Satanic cult of some kind in California," as Cheyenne Police Detective Tom Hood testified, no evidence of abuse was found.

In addition to a physical exam, there was an attempt at a forensic interview of Mirra. This was a non-starter, because the child was unable to communicate—despite the fact that Jordan insisted that her six-year-old, severely autistic son could read and write at an 8th-grade level. During the examination, she commandeered a laptop computer to "prove" that her son could communicate by taking hold of her son's hands and using his fingers to type out answers to the investigator's questions. The sight of a woman using her autistic young son's fingers to type, then claiming that her son was the person composing the messages, should've been yet another example of Jordan's derangement. But this is actually a therapy still in use among some professionals in the MPD community called "facilitated communication." This dated and repudiated technique was once believed to give voice to the autistic.[60]

At the custody hearing, Jordan's lawyer doubled down on the "conspiracy" claims and essentially challenged the court to prove that Gigi Jordan and her son were not on the run from organized crime. There was something clearly wrong with Jordan, and while even the judge admitted as much, he ruled that since the authorities couldn't definitively prove that Jordan was a danger to her son (as this would require predictive powers beyond those of the court), Jude Mirra was to be returned to his mother.

At the hearing, the judge made a statement that proved prophetic:

> One reads in the newspapers every day, it's on the national news about parents who have done horrific things to their own children.... There's one in the news yesterday about a man who checked into a hotel and drowned his three little children. I'm sure the time will come when recriminations are made saying somebody in authority should have seen this coming and acted somehow to prevent it. That's what's on everybody's mind right here. That's the elephant in the room that nobody talks about.

Ultimately, the judge ruled, "Our system doesn't work that way. You don't go arrest somebody because you're afraid they might do something."

Jude Mirra's life ended in a $2,500 per night suite at the Peninsula, a luxury hotel in midtown Manhattan. His mother had checked into the hotel on February 3, 2010, and paid cash. Earlier that day, she hired a taxi to drive her and her son around Manhattan for three hours, during rush hour, in an apparent attempt to shake the conspiracy that she believed had followed them to the East Coast.

In a feature for *Newsweek*, Alexander Nazaryan describes Jordan as wealthy and desperate. When her son was diagnosed as autistic, she pursued quack therapies that didn't promise to cure him as much as absolve him, to deny the reality of the diagnosis. It was while looking for "alternative" cures for her son that Jordan discovered Carol Crow, a Tampa-based mental health counselor who specializes in EMDR and trauma therapy. According to the *New York Post*, Crow diagnosed Jude Mirra with multiple personality disorder.[61]

"There were three separate individuals communicating by name with me," Crow testified at the murder trial, referring to the child's alleged alters. "He was clearly changing from one part to another. He used names for these parts. There was 'Killer,' the angry part. 'Eiken,' that was the child-like personality, and there was Jude." Mirra was non-verbal. He couldn't speak directly to Crow—his mother typed out his half of the conversation on a BlackBerry using "facilitated communication," providing answers that mom and therapist attributed to the boy.

Ultimately, Jude Mirra was reduced to the status of a mere prop, which the mother and the therapist used to spin their own elaborate fantasy of persecution.

Crow wasn't the only mental health professional who had failed Jude Mirra. Before flying into Wyoming in 2008, Jordan consulted Ellen Lacter, a San Diego-based therapist who specializes in trauma therapy. As Lacter recorded at the time on a state-mandated child abuse report:

> Gigi Jordan . . . reports that Jude has recently (since early, 2008) disclosed to her that Emille Tzekov (Jude's biological father who has relinquished his parental rights) abused him (Jude), including penetration, anal penetration (unknown if digital or penile), forced ingestion of feces, putting needles under his fingernails and in the webs between his fingers, choking him, and needle-pricking his chest and legs. Jude has suffered developmental delays and medical conditions that may be a direct effect of this alleged abuse. Gigi Jordan is concerned that Mr. Tzekov may be similarly abusing his one-to-two-year-old son, whom she has never met, but whom she believes exists.

Ellen Lacter is the former head of the ISST-D's Ritual Abuse/Mind Control/Organized Abuse Special Interest Group—a subgroup within the ISST-D devoted to the study of mind control and Satanic abuse conspiracies.[62] Her website, endritualabuse.org, contains a few of her articles.

They have titles like "Torture-based Mind Control: Psychological Mechanisms and Psychotherapeutic Approaches to Overcoming Mind Control" and "Guidelines to Diagnosis of Ritual Abuse/Mind Control Traumatic Stress." Since it's in her professional interest to promote these theories, it should be no surprise that she would encourage Gigi Jordan's darkest delusions.

What would have happened to Jude Mirra if, instead of encouraging his mother's delusions, these therapists would've challenged her persecution fantasies and endeavored to protect the child? We'll never know. In February 2010, Gigi Jordan killed her son with a lethal combination of Xanax, Ambien, and vodka.

After a six-week trial that the *New York Post* deemed "bizarre,"[63] Gigi Jordan was sentenced to 18 years in prison in 2015. As of this writing, the professionals who encouraged her fantasies of persecution are still practicing medicine.

When I was at the earliest stages of this story, The Satanic Temple's Lucien Greaves stressed just how pervasive this retrograde Satanic panic is. "The more you look into it," he said, "the more people you'll meet who have been affected" one way or another. Soon after that conversation, the universe proved him right. It was while reading legal documents relating to Jude Mirra that I came across the name of a relative of mine. Somehow she had happened to be in the orbit of Jude Mirra and Gigi Jordan, and when

Jordan flipped her lid (to use a clinical term), she included my relative's name as one of the suspected members of the conspiracy. I asked my relative if we could talk about the story, but she demurred, saying that "I kind of have a PTSD-type thing with it."

There were no repercussions for those responsible for the Satanic Panic, Lucien said. "Within ten years of the Salem witch trials, one of the presiding judges wrote an apology, and there was a general realization that what had happened was absolutely wrong, and in fact, that's well known today. Everybody points to the Salem witch hunts as an episode of moral panic that was completely unjustified, due to destructive mob behavior. And no such thing happened with the Satanic Panic of the 1980s and '90s—there was no censure against the practices that brought us to this point, and as we see at the ISST-D, these practices still carry on, and in a sanctioned way."

And you wouldn't even know it, unless it affects you or someone in your family.

"It's really distressing," he continues. "It does seem like we run the risk currently of degenerating into a new Satanic Panic. When people can take things like Pizzagate seriously, you know there's something seriously wrong."

8

I was still looking for an ending to this story several months after meeting Colin Ross in Chicago. In the meantime, I tried to arrange a visit to his home city of Dallas so we could talk face-to-face, but our schedules didn't line up. The best I could do was give him a phone call. I didn't expect any stunning revelations from our exit interview, but I did want to know what Ross thought of his former patient, Roma Hart.

Before getting to Roma, we probably spent 30 minutes talking about "therapeutic neutrality," a subject that seems to come up in most of his interviews. It could be said that this is his major clinical insight: When a patient reveals repressed memories, Ross suspends judgment. Whether they're memories of things that have actually happened or not doesn't matter, he says. Indeed, he claims that to even judge something as impossible (even when it clearly is) could be damaging to the therapist's relationship with the patient.

"The thing that's different about me is, based on the research [into government mind control], I say it's possible that these events took place. Because there's all this type of experimentation that's been done along these lines."

It seems to me that you can only practice this kind of therapeutic neutrality if there is a chance in hell that the patient's claims *could be* true. What does it say about Colin Ross that he refuses to dismiss stories about large-scale intergenerational Satanic abuse cults or things like the Monarch program outright? Perhaps, in Colin Ross's hands, therapeutic neutrality is little more than a way to put a reasonable spin on some very unreasonable beliefs.

"Most of these 'false memory' people," Ross said, referring to the False Memory Syndrome Foundation and his other critics, "are not actually doing therapy with people who are describing these kinds of trauma histories." In treatment, "you can't just tell people 'your memories aren't real, I don't believe you,' and have them stay in treatment. It's just not going to happen. And you can have catastrophic reactions, like they get suicidal and cut themselves and get admitted to hospital." In other words, memory researchers like Elizabeth Loftus need to get out of their ivory towers of controlled, scientific studies and talk to some actual mind control victims.

Therapeutic neutrality was stretched to the breaking point in a Texas courtroom in the late 1990s when Ross and a number of his colleagues were sued by an ex-patient named Martha Ann Tyo (née Hurt).

"If you treated a patient who thought he was Napoleon,

would you write down in great detail all his battle plans and how he made his uniforms and where he stored the horses, and would you fill up dozens and dozens and dozens of pages of what Napoleon planned to do with his men?" Attorney Chris Barden asked Mary Ellen Grundman, who treated Hurt at Charter Hospital in Plano, Texas, where Colin Ross was the head of the MPD unit.

Grundman said no, she would not.

It seems to me that this is precisely what MPD therapists like Ross are doing when they root around in their patient's psyches, working out elaborate schematics of their fragmented personalities.

Tyo's story is detailed in an October 1999 *Dallas Observer* story by Ann Zimmerman titled "Cult of Madness."

In 1990, Martha Ann Tyo was still known as Martha Hurt, a 32-year-old housewife with three adopted kids, a history of medical problems, and a troubled marriage. She was understandably depressed and sought out marriage counseling. Eventually, she found herself under the care of a trauma therapist named Dr. Stephen Ash, who convinced Tyo that she had multiple personality disorder and repressed memories of Satanic ritual abuse. Therapy with Ash consisted of hypnosis and play-acting alleged past incidents of abuse. At one point, Tyo heard a story in group therapy about rituals involving snakes, only to subsequently recover her own ritual abuse memories involving snakes. She also recovered memories of having seen a girl murdered and her heart cut out of her chest. According to

Zimmerman, this particular story comes from *The Courage to Heal* by Ellen Bass and Laura Davis, one of the keystone texts of the recovered memory movement (and, from what I've heard, a common source of "recovered" memories).

In January 1992, Tyo was admitted to Charter Hospital in Plano, where her alters multiplied. According to Zimmerman, "at one point she believed she had almost 200 of them. And, not coincidentally," as her therapy was being overseen by Colin Ross, "she suddenly began remembering times in her youth when she had been programmed by government operatives."

According to Ross, a person with a Satanic abuse background is more likely to suffer effects of the repressed trauma on certain days of the year.[*] In Charter Hospital, Zimmerman writes, Tyo "was given a copy of a satanic calendar that listed important satanic holidays" [sic]. If she was feeling unwell on a particular day, she was told, it was probably because it was the anniversary of a Satanic holiday on which she had been abused in the past.

Tyo and her husband had adopted three children because she couldn't have children of her own. But under Ross's care, she was told that she had given birth to six children in her cultic past, starting at age 9.

"All my life, I wanted to have a baby," she told Zimmerman. "The most devastating thing you could tell

---

[*] I've heard Ross make this claim a number of times, most recently on the June 16, 2018 episode of *The Opperman Report* podcast, available at: https://youtu.be/kfhZCiarDNw

me was that I had a baby and killed it, ate it, and drank the baby's blood," which was precisely what she was told by her therapists. "I thought I was the most evil thing on the face of the earth and didn't deserve to live."

In 1998, Tyo came to realize, as the fog of drugs and bad therapy began to lift, that her "recovered" past consisted of little more than fantasies suggested and reified by her caregivers. With the lawyer and psychologist R. Christopher Barden acting as her counsel, the case went to trial and was eventually settled out of court "for a hefty undisclosed amount."[64]

In an email, Barden explained the problem with settlements in malpractice cases. "Ninety-eight percent of all civil litigation settles with confidentiality provisions that hide the truth about what happened," he wrote. Due to the nature of Tyo's settlement, she can no longer talk to journalists. That is why her legal team publicized her story while the case was still in court.

"We worked to get the news media story out about Dr. Ross's work and colleagues in the Martha Hurt case," Barden continued, "precisely because we knew that that case—like so many others—would settle with confidentiality provisions."

According to Roma Hart, the only reason that we know her story at all is that her case was dismissed after having wound its way through the Canadian court system for over a decade. A settlement was never reached, so she never signed a confidentiality agreement.

"I am on welfare disability," Hart told Lucien Greaves

in a recent interview. "The only money I could raise for lawyers was just through begging people that I was given contact numbers for." A small, impromptu network of victims and critics of Colin Ross had formed over the years, and it was through the help of this network that Roma was able to scrape together the money to "drag" her case "through the system for 11 years, with 4 different lawyers." Eventually, the case was dismissed due to delays caused by one of her lawyers' mismanagement.[65]

"What's going on with Roma Hart?" I eventually asked Ross. I sort of blurted it out, really. I wanted to know what he would say when confronted with the name of his most famous patient (aside from Roseanne Barr).

He was nonplussed.

"I worked with her when I was in Canada," he said, "which I left in 1991. The therapy with her ended in 1990. In 1994, she was on *The Sally Jessy Raphael Show* with [U.C. Berkeley sociologist and Pulitzer Prize winner] Richard Ofshe, who then talked her into filing a lawsuit against me, which went on for quite a while but was dismissed."

The episode of *Sally* that he refers to was first broadcast in 1993[66] and can be found on YouTube. (The version I found was given the title: "Dr. Colin Ross - Trump Card | Mind Control|Marijuana|** Coast To Coast AM|EOD 47.")

Ross goes unnamed in this episode, which begins with Hart relating the story that she told me, and that she has told many people over the years (anyone who would listen, really). She describes how she had met the therapist while looking for a doctor to sign off on a form for her unemployment; how she had played along when he asked her about her alternate personalities; how, through a combination of hypnosis, drugs, and bad therapy, her sanity was taken from her.

Of course, Ross sees it differently. "She just has a tremendous number of fantastic stories that are impossible," he said. "Like, I made her believe that she had an alien baby, and the aliens came back and took the babies away. She claims that that's what I made her believe. She claimed that I made her believe that she was a victim of CIA mind control. The CIA was never mentioned by me or her throughout the entire therapy. If you go through all of her allegations, it's almost like Munchausen's level—obviously not true stories."

This last statement struck me as odd, coming from the author of *Military Mind Control*.

"People who actually have obvious, florid delusional disorders," Ross said, "it's irrelevant to the false memory controversy. Nobody in the trauma field is doing therapy with those kinds of people, end of discussion."

But he *did* conduct therapy with Roma Hart for several years.

"She's just a very disturbed person," according to Ross. "And the false memory people use her all the time."

If Roma came in as a patient today, I asked, and if she described extraterrestrial offspring and CIA mind control, would he follow this therapeutic neutrality principle?

"Not on the space aliens part, no."

I guess some things are too weird to admit, even for Colin Ross.

"I've only met maybe 2 or 3 people who claimed alien abduction in my entire career," he said. "And even that's not totally, totally impossible."

9

On December 4, 2016, a 28-year old man from North Carolina named Edgar Maddison Welch entered a bar and pizza restaurant called Comet Ping Pong in Washington D.C.[67] For weeks, he had been hearing about "Pizzagate," a conspiracy theory which maintained that the Democratic Party, when it wasn't busy blowing elections, was operating a pedophile sex trafficking ring. This was around the time that John Podesta's emails were hacked, and online conspiracy theorists felt that they were able to "decode" the email messages, which ultimately revealed that Comet Ping Pong was the epicenter of Democratic sex trafficking. According to the conspiracy theory, Comet Ping Pong had a basement, and in the basement, children were kept for dark, perverted purposes.

What is a good man, a religious man, to do when faced with a brutal truth such as this? If you're Mr. Welch, you grab a shotgun, a handgun, and an AR-15 semi-automatic rifle, and drive to the nation's capital to investigate.

Welch entered the restaurant on a Sunday afternoon. As patrons fled the scene in terror, he found a locked door. He fired into it three times with his AR-15, with the intention of descending the stairs that lay on the other side of the door into the bowels of the establishment, fighting for his life, if need be—and fighting for the lives of the children he believed to be held captive.

But there were no captive children. And there was no set of stairs, and no basement—just a storage closet. Welch surrendered to police, and luckily no one was injured.[68] In March 2017 he pleaded guilty to federal charges of transporting a firearm over state lines and assault with a dangerous weapon. He is currently serving a four-year prison sentence.[69]

In an interview with *The New York Times* shortly after the incident, Welch admitted that his reconnaissance of Comet Ping Pong was bone-headed, but he stopped short of denying the reality of the Pizzagate conspiracy.

"I just wanted to do some good," he said, "and went about it the wrong way."[70]

It was about 18 months after the shooting when I stopped by Comet Ping Pong on a Sunday evening to try the pizza (it was fine) and drink a couple over-priced beers. I guess I expected a pub — a poorly lit, smoke-filled room with a stage for bands. Comet Ping Pong, it turns out, is a family restaurant. It's the kind of place where you wouldn't feel weird letting your kids run around unattended while you ate dinner. On the night that I visited, it was packed; children probably outnumbered adults 3-to-1. On the PA system, it was the Eighties channel on Spotify: Devo, Bowie, Joan Jett's version of "Crimson and Clover." In the back room, where bands play on some evenings, a foosball table sat on a pair of beer kegs. And, of course, there were the ping pong tables, where children tried (with varying levels of success) to clear the net. After dinner, I believe I found the locked door that Welch had fired into. It has been repaired, all traces of gunfire effectively erased.

The trials of Roma Hart and Martha Ann Tyo show what happens when conspiracy culture practices medicine, just like the shooting at Comet Ping Pong shows what happens when conspiracy culture picks up a gun.

This story has largely been about what certain people believe to be real versus what science or history tells us is real. The pseudoscience of recovered memory therapy, for instance, and the pseudo-history of CIA mind control experiments. Taken together, all of these falsehoods have created a pseudo-reality. In individuals like Edgar Maddison Welch, pseudo-reality and *real*-reality collide. One wonders why this doesn't happen more often, and why more people haven't been hurt.

But people *have* been hurt. Jude Mirra lost his life because the therapists that his mother consulted with were living in this pseudo-reality, one where it was more plausible that some sort of Satanic conspiracy was stalking her child than the obvious explanation—Mirra was autistic, and his mother was disturbed. And for a good many years, Roma Hart lived in a pseudo-reality where individuals contained multiple personalities, personalities implanted by government programs designed to create mind control slaves. As a result, she lost her family, and she lost precious years of her life.

You need only spend an hour or two on Facebook or Twitter to see that an increasing proportion of Americans are being swept up in pseudo-reality. Politicians like Donald Trump and conspiracy entrepreneurs like Alex Jones have learned that there is both wealth and political power to be gained by promoting this pseudo-reality. (That is not to say that they're the first people to figure this out, of course; they're just two egregious, contemporary examples.)

Take the example of the Satanic Panic. As the 1980s turned into the 1990s, the media and the criminal justice system seemed to realize that recovered memory therapy was unscientific and that Satanic ritual abuse claims based on recovered memories were bogus. The talk shows switched to other topics, the lawsuits resulting from recovered memories dropped off.

But, "the theory of repressed memory did not go away," Mark Pendergrast wrote in his book *Memory Warp*. "It just went underground." Pendergrast and psychology professor Lawrence Patihis recently concluded a large-scale survey of over 2,300 people to try and gauge popular beliefs regarding recovered memories.[71] Pendergrast and Patihis have found that, when adjusted for gender, ethnicity, and race, over 4 percent of the population believes that they have "discovered" past abuse through recovered memory therapy. "If that is representative of the adult U.S. population," Pendergrast writes, "that means that over 9 million people in this country have come to believe that they suffered childhood abuse but completely forgot about it until they sought psychotherapy."

In other words, if the numbers are correct, there are an estimated 9 million people in this country who have been forcibly separated from reality by incompetent or unscrupulous mental health professionals. One has to assume that for these residents of pseudo-reality, there are plenty who are capable of actions every bit as looney as those of Edgar Maddison Welch.

Sometimes I think that conspiracy theorists—whether they are the consumers of social media fake news or patients of recovered memory pseudo-therapy—are the canaries in the coal mine of society, the sensitive souls who are first affected by (and who come to embody) the tensions that are the inevitable product of our ever-changing culture, with its ever-increasing rate of change. Indeed, in the case of the Satanic Panic, that moral panic that popularized and normalized things like Satanic ritual abuse and multiple personality disorder, we can see precisely what cultural forces were at work.

"Satanic cult rumors," according to SUNY sociologist Jeffrey S. Victor, "[arise] out of concrete sources of shared social stress," particularly in "areas which manifest particularly high rates of economic decline and family disintegration."[72] In the following passage, published in 1993, Victor could be talking about Ronald Reagan's

America then, or he could be predicting Donald Trump's America now:

> Rumors, allegations, and claims about satanism [sic] may also be a symptom of an emerging moral crisis in American society as a whole, as increasing numbers of people experience the effects of economic stress and family disintegration. If the economic decline of America accelerates as more and more well-paid blue-collar jobs disappear, it is likely that people will fantasize more conspirational threats and seek to find more scapegoats for their anxieties.[73]

Sitting at the bar at Comet Ping Pong, I asked the bartender if he was a witness to the shooting. He tells me that he wasn't, he had that day off, but that he's suffered his fair share of harassment by conspiracy theorists nonetheless. Everyone at Comet has.

"They call every day," he said.

Who calls? I asked. What do they say? He doesn't answer my question, not exactly, but he does keep talking.

"They're not from around here. They think that Washington D.C. is the place where every terrible thing in the world comes from."

His manager chimed in: "Every day we have to answer questions like yours," he said. It's a tense moment. He's smiling, but it is not a friendly smile. It's a smile that says he's ready to attack.

Just like Roma Hart and Martha Ann Tyo, the shell-shocked staff of Comet Ping Pong are victims of conspiracy theory culture. They stand at the edge of a rippling wave that began late last century when Americans started to believe in a tin-pot Satan behind any number of social ills. Pizzagate is the most recent manifestation of this, but it won't be the last.

I knew that the guy behind the bar didn't want to hear any of that, so I paid for my drink, left a good tip, and got the hell out of there.

What else could I do?

. . . AND OTHER STORIES

The Rise of the Conspiracy Creeps

(*From* The Conspiracy Review, *March 31, 2015)*

> "For many years I sincerely believed that an extraterrestrial threat existed and that it was the most important driving force behind world events. I was wrong and for that I most deeply and humbly apologize." — Bill Cooper

The conspiracist M. William Cooper (but you can call him Bill) was born in 1943. According to his bio, he was a Vietnam-era veteran of both the Navy and the Air Force, and later some sort of photographer, before making a name for himself in the "UFOlogist" counterculture of the 1980s with extraordinary tales of extraterrestrial races, secret human populations on the moon, and a predilection for championing known hoaxes (such as the infamous Protocols of the Elders of Zion) as documentary evidence of a worldwide global conspiracy of the rich and powerful, intent on enslaving every last one of us. Cooper even had a term for you and I, the everyday schlubs who refuse to see the truth in his message and join him on his crusade. We were mere "sheeple," he'd say—a portmanteau of *sheep* and *people*—"cattle by choice and by consent."

"I read while in Naval Intelligence," he claimed in his book *Behold A Pale Horse*, "that at least once a year, maybe more, two nuclear submarines meet beneath the polar icecap and mate together at an airlock. Representatives of the Soviet Union meet with the Policy Committee of the Bilderberg Group. The Russians are given the script for their next performance. Items on the agenda include the combined efforts in the secret space program."

The secret space program, of course, is the operation that has established a military presence on the moon and Mars.

Cooper continues: "I now have in my possession official NASA photographs of a moonbase in the crater Copernicus."

Conspiracy theorists all tend to draw on a common pool of elements, but few could match Cooper in his ability to account for almost every fringe idea out there. The effect, for those who accepted his message, must have been profound—like having the veil lifted from your eyes and, for the first time, seeing the world as it really is. Even though I thought the whole thing was nuts, his was still a compelling and highly entertaining alternate universe; one where every day the forces of good and evil were locked in conflict, where every question could be explained by invoking the Illuminati or the New World Order. Cooper described a world where everything had its place and everything was significant. No one—not the History Channel, not Steven Spielberg—could make history come alive quite like him. Even if his "history" was often no more real than the one where Kirk and Spock are caught infiltrating the Space Nazis in violation of the Prime Directive.

April 19, 1993 was a cool spring morning. My dad drove me out to some shitty small town somewhere out in Erie County to apply for a job at a mill or cardboard box factory or something. It was my senior year at General McLane High School, and most of my graduating class was getting ready to either join the military, move on to a state school of higher education, or go work in a plant somewhere. None of those options appealed to me, so the guidance counselor at Vo-Tech set me up with an interview for a gig as a COBOL programmer—which I was totally unqualified for. As we made the trip in silence, I prayed to God that I wouldn't get the job. And for the first time in my life, I'm pleased to say, the power of prayer worked.

I still remember sitting in the car on the way home, hearing the news that the ATF was rolling up to the Branch Davidian compound near Waco, Texas, in armored vehicles and filling it with tear gas. I didn't know what to think about it, except that it didn't sound too good. Wasn't that place full of kids? It soon turned out that we were ear-witnessing a slow-motion, cold-blooded murder on AM news radio. In total, 87 people died (28 were under the age of 21) for no good reason. With the benefit of hindsight, it's obvious that the massacre was an FBI fuck-up of monstrous proportions, and that the raid itself was unwarranted.

Throughout the 51-day siege, I was captivated by Bill Cooper's radio show, *The Hour of the Time*. Each episode began with an air raid siren, then a sort of poem read in a weird robot voice (which bears considerable resemblance to Vincent Price's opening monologue on the cult-classic Canadian kids show *The Hilarious House of Frightenstein*). Add the marching of jackboot thugs, screams, and dogs barking, and you're primed for nightmares before Cooper even opens his mouth.

The show's formula was strikingly similar to the one that Alex Jones follows today. Essentially, the facts of the siege were bent beyond recognition in an effort to make the tragedy fit his pet New World Order conspiracy theory. (To give credit where it's due, Cooper was one of the first to report that the Branch Davidians were a mostly harmless Christian sect with ties to the community, which turned out to be true. He also said that the he caught the ATF on video doing some sort of Satanic-Illuminati rain dance around the smoldering remains of the compound, which has yet to be definitively proven.)

Cooper died soon after the terror attacks of September 11, 2001. He had been holed up in his home in a small town in Arizona for a number of years, wanted by the feds for tax evasion. Like many of those militia-types, he had done the calculations and decided that, through a series of regulatory perambulations I could never quite fathom (including something about writing "the united States of America" with a lowercase "united") that the income tax was unconstitutional, and therefore he simply wouldn't pay it. This, of course, made wild Bill a criminal, by definition. The feds knew where he was, but they didn't go after him. The last thing they wanted, after Waco, was another bloodbath.

In the end, Bill's death came at the hands of local law enforcement. Responding to an aggravated assault complaint, they tried to coax him out of his yard sometime before noon on November 5, 2001. A gunfight ensued: one officer was critically wounded, and Cooper was killed. Since then, the aftershocks of two major cultural forces—the September 11 attacks and the growing power of the internet—have splintered his message into innumerable pieces and scattered them throughout our society. Everything from the 9/11 truthers to the yuppie war against vaccination, from the current crop of post-apocalyptic, anti-authoritarian Young Adult novels to the absurd practice of taking loaded assault rifles into Chipotle and Instagramming about it later; the doomsday rhetoric thrown around by the likes of Glenn Beck and the late Michael Ruppert all contain somewhere within it the DNA of Bill Cooper.

The most well known descendant of Bill Cooper is Alex Jones. The former high school football player's star was on the rise at the time of Cooper's death, a fact that didn't please the volatile host of *The Hour of the Time*. In fact, Cooper devoted one full hour-long episode to Alex Jones, during which he edited down some of Jones's radio broadcasts to make them somehow sound even more insane than they actually were.

On December 31, 1999, on live radio, Alex Jones reported the Y2K meltdown of society in real-time—as it played out only in his fevered imagination. The United States military invaded Austin, Texas and began preparations for martial law as nuclear power plants began failing all over the country. A young upstart named Vladimir Putin, "raging with power," had his finger on the trigger, hastening nuclear war. It was basically *War of the Worlds*, except that the host of the program clearly believed his own bullshit.

It might be utterly foolish to look for a motive inside someone's mad ravings, but that never stopped Bill Cooper. According to Cooper, the Alex Jones Y2K freak out had "the smell of a setup." In other words, he was asking: just who is Alex Jones really working for? The CIA? Mossad? The Illuminati?

All these conspiracy creeps are con artists, and by income alone Alex Jones is the biggest creep out there. To be honest, I'm not sure that he even knows that he's a con artist—that's the extent of his deceit. Contrary to the conspiracist infighting, Alex Jones is not working for the "global elite" or some CommuNazi New World Order. He's working for himself, and he's doing quite well. As of 2013, The Alex Jones Show is broadcast daily on over 160 radio stations, and the take from all his properties is estimated to be at least $10 million a year.[74]

Americans love their conspiracy theories. Looking for the hidden influences behind the scenes is the natural impulse of a wary, irreverent population that's been conditioned to think for itself—even if it doesn't always have access to the resources to make the most informed decisions. And that's a healthy impulse. But it becomes pathological when the most gullible of us get whipped into a frenzy by a millionaire that's selling himself as some sort of populist folk hero. In this respect, Alex Jones and the establishment he rails against have an awful lot in common.

The Boston Marathon Bombing 'Truth' Movement

(*From* Pando Daily, *May 15, 2015)*

The photos were all taken within milliseconds of each other, and they're all very similar—if not practically the same.

A woman wearing a backpack purse gets pulled away from the danger by someone wearing a white sweatshirt. Two people on the ground, one wearing a blue windbreaker, the other wearing sunglasses, are huddled together. Faces are twisted in what appear to be agony, or shock, or incomprehension. In the upper left hand corner, if you recognize the light grey sweatshirt with the dark gray sleeves, you can make out Jeff Bauman, the double-amputee who famously helped investigators identify Dzhokar and Tamerlan Tsarnaev in the aftermath of the Boston Marathon bombing.[75]

These photos were taken by Ben Thorndike, an amateur photographer and self-described "marathon junkie" who spent April 15, 2013, snapping pictures of the finish line of the Boston Marathon. They capture some of the clearest shots of the infamous attack and its immediate aftermath, and in the days following the the bombing they were featured on NBC Nightly News, CNN, and a number of other outlets.

Considering the magnitude of the attack, the media attention is to be expected.

What Thorndike did not expect was the attention he and his photographs would receive from conspiracy theorists around the world. To them, the photos were the smoking gun that proved the Boston Marathon bombing never happened.

On April 8, Dzhokar Tsarnaev was found guilty of the bombing that killed three people and injured 264 others. His life now hangs in the balance, as jurors decide whether he should face the death penalty or life in prison.[76] To jurors, Dzhokar's guilt was a foregone conclusion. But for a small crowd of conspiracy theorists, the defense team's admission of guilt was just the latest in a series of lies told to the public in service of a larger, false narrative.

There's no modern conspiracy theory that's more counterintuitive or flat-out mean than the belief that the victims of the Tsarnaev brothers (roughly 260 injured and three killed) were merely con artists or "crisis actors." According to this theory, the dead and wounded are the real criminals, working in league with a secret government to hoodwink the American people.

On race day, Thorndike was positioned in the window at his firm, Feingold O'Keeffe Capital, documenting the action with his DSLR camera.

"I was looking toward the finish line, and right before me there was a huge explosion, a fireball, a deafening boom," he told the *Boston Globe*. "I basically knew it was a bomb. My gut instinct said it was horrific, and my brain said to aim the camera and push the button. I started shooting almost instantaneously."[77]

After he got home and found what his camera had captured, he contacted a friend in broadcast media. The reaction was instantaneous, and overwhelming. News trucks arrived at his home. The phone started ringing, didn't stop for weeks. At the peak of the media's interest, Thorndike began declining interviews. ABC, Fox News, and multiple print magazines got the cold shoulder, he says. A producer from *Entertainment Tonight* went so far as to camp out on his doorstep at 9:00 PM one night and refuse to leave until Thorndike consented to an interview (his plan didn't work).

That's where things would have remained, had Thorndike not come across something called *The Memory Hole Blog*. Founded and maintained by a Florida Atlantic University professor (and unaffiliated conspiracy theorist) named James Tracy,[*] the site is a newswire for all the latest

* After years of embarrassing the university, especially through his promoting absurd Sandy Hook conspiracy theories, Tracy was finally terminated on December 16, 2015. *News.com.au* December 18, 2015. http://archive.fo/JTU2X

conspiracy bugbears. What Thorndike found published there beggared belief: "proof" that the government had faked the Boston Marathon bombing, and that all the so-called victims were instead government contractors. Finding the allegations almost as upsetting as the event itself, he emailed Tracy in an attempt to set the record straight.

"You wrote an article about my marathon photos that is filled with inaccuracies," Thorndike wrote. Why hadn't Tracy contacted him before publishing the story? "I would have thought a disciplined author would seek out sources and ask questions before leaping to conclusions and putting them in writing." (Although I've been in touch with Thorndike, he's denied multiple requests for interviews; from here on out, I'm quoting from a batch of emails that Tracy sent me.)

From here, a maddening volley of emails ensued. Tracy seemed to believe that the photos not only revealed a government plot, but that they also somehow fingered Thorndike as a co-conspirator. "I am also especially interested in your most opportune positioning at the site of the event as it transpired," Tracy replied.

"Opportune?" asked Thorndike, incredulous. "How about you, Mr. Tracy, walk to a window and have a bomb go off underneath you, and then we'll see if you think of it as 'opportune.'"

Later, over the phone, Tracy told me he's "not even sure who Ben Thorndike is. I'm not sure as to whether or not he might somehow be a government player." As Tracy explains it, the attack at the Boston Marathon was a training exercise for government operatives. It was the next evolution of something like Urban Shield, a mock terrorist attack conducted by a private company meant to test the abilities of local, state, and federal responders.

"There were people that were brought in, to more or less act as injured parties and deceased parties," Tracy said. "There have been studies that have been done on [Thorndike's] photographs that show the mechanics of the event itself," that ostensibly prove that the bombing never happened.

Of course, there haven't been studies—just rants on blogs and forums. But for plenty of people (too many people, in fact) that's evidence enough.

Each generation seems to have its favored conspiracy-type. In the 1960s and 1970s, conspiracy theories tended to be bureaucratic-martial, as exemplified by the examination and re-examination and re-re-examination of ballistics evidence in the JFK-MLK-RFK assassinations, and the endless cross-referencing of the Warren Commission findings. Over the next twenty years we began to see more of a sci-fi, *X-Files*-flavored kookiness, with alien abductions and that sort of thing.

After 9/11, things took on a more sinister cast. Individuals began doubting some very basic, rock solid facts. The World Trade Center, it was said, was brought down by explosives—because the planes the nation saw that morning were actually holograms. As for Sandy Hook

Elementary, it's claimed that the school had been closed for a number of years prior to the massacre. Like the victims of Boston, the kids at Newtown were all purportedly actors. This perspective requires a distinct lack of empathy on the part of the conspiracist. You can wallow in this mindset for yourself by looking at Thorndike's pictures and trying to see in them what James Tracy sees:

> **Frame six:** On the left we see the the man with a hood setting up the fake leg wound prosthetics... The woman is acting as a shield covering what's happening.

> **Frame eight:** The prosthetics are in place. Amidst all this chaos seconds after the explosion the hooded man takes the time to put on his sunglasses which is a signal.

> **Frame nine:** With sunglasses now on the hooded man and the woman make eye contact, signal received.

> **Frame eleven:** After recieving [sic] the go signal the woman makes an open hand gesture the direction both of them are looking, signaling the staged injuries are in place for cameras…

> **Frame fourteen:** The woman turns her head right but is still holding up that open palm signal with

her left hand. The hooded man again busies himself pouring fake blood on the pavement behind the woman. The amputee has both fake injuries in the air now. There is still no blood on his legs, his skin above the injury is clean and dry.

Frame twenty: The fake blood and prosthetics are in place. The amputee gives an open hand gesture along with the woman to bring the cameras in. We're now twenty frames in and still not a drop of fresh blood from a double leg amputation. His legs are dry, the woman is dry and unscathed. Both are making the same hand gesture.

It takes a cold, cynical person to look at clear pictures of a veritable slaughter and see actors engaged in a conspiracy. (Either that, or some kind of idiot.)

I assured Tracy that I saw something very different than he did. Then, I asked him: who orchestrated the alleged Boston Marathon bombing hoax?

The answer, as you probably have guessed, is Obama. He's the puppet master, directing his minions in the Department of Homeland Security.

But why?

"There's actually a study that was conducted," he explains, "and I know that there's got to be more than one.

But the Department [sic] of Naval Intelligence* was studying Twitter and Facebook, how the event took shape on social media, alongside mainstream media.

In other words, Tracy would like you to believe that the federal government traumatized the entire nation at considerable expense, not only as a training exercise, but to see what people would tweet about it.

I came away from my conversation with James Tracy, the academic conspiracist and self-styled public intellectual, with the distinct impression that he thinks very highly of himself. And compared to some of his colleagues across the country, Tracy almost comes across as a reasonable human being. In Chicago, for instance, there's Cass Ingram (also known as Cassim K., Dr. K., and Kaasem Khaleel), a disgraced former osteopath that marries the Boston Marathon bombing conspiracy to classic, old fashioned anti-Semitism. His invective is aimed squarely at Tsarnaev's victims, branding them liars, Satanists, and Zionists. Then there's the pseudonymous BuelahMan, a self-described "Mississippi redneck" who "don't trust Jews." He was one of the first to pounce on the "analysis" of Thorndike's photos that Tracy bases his theories on.

For a conspiracy enthusiast such as myself, it's always disappointing when I stumble upon a new theory only to

---

* There is no Department of Naval Intelligence. I suppose that he meant the Office of Naval Intelligence.

discover that it's a rehash of something as lame as old fashioned anti-Semitism. Unfortunately, says Mark Fenster, the author of *Conspiracy Theories: Secrecy and Power in American Culture*, this is practically inevitable. Whenever there's a national tragedy such as Boston, he recently told me, "there's a typical pattern, and all conspiracies tend to fall into that fairly quickly."

According to Fenster, a conspiracy theory (whether it's promoted as real, or the plot of a movie like *JFK* or *Bob Roberts*) is a "generic, stock narrative" that serves as a "framework for filmmakers and conspiracy theorists." In this light, conspiracy creeps like James Tracy are shown for what they really are: hack filmmakers, working without a crew. On one level, this should come as a surprise to no one. Just about every conspiracy theory, no matter which shocking "revelations" it may contain, has the same stale plot structure.

To the victims of the Tsarnaev brothers, there's nothing worthwhile about James Tracy's work. Indeed, the only thing that's truly revelatory about Tracy is the fact that he's convinced people to believe his rap.

In their correspondence, Tracy had the nerve to ask Thorndike if he was "truly convinced" the the bombing was "an authentic event?" And "If so, why?" It's a question that needn't be dignified with a response, but Thorndike, good sport that he is, responded nonetheless.

"I saw the explosion," he wrote back. "Literally. I saw the huge ball of fire, heard the deafening noise, watched the smoke billowing upwards and saw people knocked to the ground like bowling pins."

It's been several years since the attack, and in that time Thorndike has met a number of people who were either wounded that day, or had family members who were wounded. Of all these people, he says, "none of them doubt what they saw."

The Moon Is Its Own Light

(From The Kernel, *September 20, 2015)*

In the year 1543, the Pope teamed up with Copernicus, the Church of England, and possibly Aristotle (who, inconveniently, had died in 322 B.C.) to convince unsuspecting Europeans that, despite the Earth's obvious flatness, it's actually a sphere, and that the sun is the center of the solar system. In the years since, the usual bad guys—Catholics, Jews, and international bankers—have jealously guarded the secret of the flat Earth. And with the birth of the space age, NASA (basically a joint project between the Freemasons and the Nazis) got involved. That, at least, is the story according to the Flat Earth Truthers, a small but vocal group who believe that the world is flat, and that this knowledge is the key to understanding who really runs the world.

Eric Dubay is arguably the most visible Flat Earth Truther. On his Blogger bio, Dubay describes himself as just another 30-something American cool dude, "living in Thailand where I teach Yoga and Wing Chun part-time while exposing the New World Order full-time." That work involves publishing exposés like "Dinosaur Hoax – Dinosaurs Never Existed!" and "Adolf Hitler vs. The Jew World Order." That's right—the *Jew* World Order.

Dubay's latest e-book is titled *200 Proofs Earth is Not a Spinning Ball*. In it, he lays out the basics of modern flat Earth theory. The moon, he writes, is a self-luminescent, semi-transparent object, not solid at all. The International Space Station is really a drone or a hologram (like the planes that hit the World Trade Center, I guess). And the Earth itself is a disc, like the emblem on the flag of the United Nations, or an old Beatles record. The North Pole is in the center of the disc, where you secure it to the turntable, and traveling south takes you to the beginning of Track 1 ("Taxman"). Antarctica, instead of being a continent, is a wall of ice that rings 'round the edge of the disc, holding the oceans in place.

According to Dubay, this is all common sense. And it was once common knowledge, before the world's secret rulers brainwashed everyone. But as Brian Dunning notes on his *Skeptoid* podcast, the idea that our ancient ancestors believed in a flat Earth is actually a modern myth.[78] For as long as people have been observing and measuring the Earth, it seems, it's been understood that we live on a globe. Pythagoras, Aristotle, Euclid—none of them doubted this. Eratosthenes, a Greek geographer and mathematician who died 200 years before the birth of Christ, determined the circumference of the Earth within 2 percent of its exact measurement.

This is pretty much where the flat Earth debate ended, regardless of what you may have heard about Christopher Columbus. That is, until the 1800s, when an Englishman named Samuel Rowbotham (known by the pen name Parallax) decided that since his Bible said that the Earth is flat, then indeed the earth has to be flat. To prove it, he ran around England with his surveying equipment, taking measurements that he then twisted to "prove" whatever he wished—the definition of pseudoscience.

Parallax was a major influence on the Flat Earth Society, founded in 1956 by another Englishman, Samuel Shenton. After Shenton's death in 1971, the society (then little more than a somewhat amusing newsletter) was taken over by an American, Charles K. Johnson. Like those before him, Johnson's flat Earth beliefs were firmly rooted in the Bible. "If earth were a ball spinning in space," he told *Newsweek* in 1984, "there would be no up or down." And if there is no up or down, Jesus couldn't have ascended into heaven.

According to Rich Hopkins, a flat Earth truther known as "MrThriveAndSurvive" to the 10,000-plus subscribers of his YouTube channel, "the Aztecs, Mayans, Sumerians, the Bible, the Koran—all of 'em said that the Earth is flat and not moving. All of 'em!" Even today, he says, "Many places in the east don't believe we're on a round spinning ball. It's mostly a Western phenomenon. The Muslim nations, they know it's a joke that we went to the moon."

Except, of course, that isn't true—and it's highly insulting to the larger, non-Western portion of the world.

Hopkins says that he became aware of the flat Earth this spring. He made the discovery while conducting his version of scientific research on YouTube. At the time, he was just another prepper, pushing colloidal silver cures and preaching the imminent collapse of society to a small YouTube audience. But then he saw a newscast from Michigan about something called a superior mirage, an optical illusion resulting from a weather event known as an inversion. In this case, the mirage was a tiny, upside-down reflection of the Chicago skyline that appeared, Fatima-like, over Lake Michigan.

"I've always been a meteorologist and a weatherman," says Hopkins, referring to his service as an aerographer's mate in the Navy in the 1980s. "I've always been into science to some degree anyways. ... I was paid for it for four years in the Navy, so I call myself a meteorologist."

Spotting the Chicago skyline from the shores of Lake Michigan called into question everything he thought he knew about how the universe works, so Hopkins began experimenting. First he took a pair of binoculars out into the desert near his home in Phoenix, Arizona. Driving around, crudely surveying the landscape, he could see for miles and miles. That was too far, he thought, but only if you assumed a curved Earth. If the Earth was flat, he reasoned, seeing so far wouldn't be a problem.

Once convinced that the Earth was flat, Hopkins started thinking about the cosmos, and what he refers to as "the biblical thing."

"The Bible says the moon is its own light," he explains, seemingly referring to a description in Genesis of "the greater light to rule the day and the lesser light to rule the night." That set him to pondering. "So I went online one day and tried to search, 'What is the difference between moonlight and sunlight, the properties?' You won't find anything. You won't find a thing. And you mean nobody's ever studied this? I can't believe that."

So he conducted an experiment using an old table, a black leather wallet, and a laser thermometer. On a clear night, he used the table to shield half of the wallet from the moonlight. Measuring both sides of his wallet with the thermometer, he determined that the moonlit portion was cooler than the half that lay under the table. He concluded, as any reasonable person might, that the moon had to be a star. More evidence that we are being lied to about the true nature of space, and the true nature of our planet.

In the three months since Hopkins started promoting flat Earth theories, his subscriber count has increased fourfold. I'm going to suggest that this newfound popularity—and the popularity of what should be a long-dead idea—is only one small symptom of what Michael Moore famously called the "fictitious times" that we live in. As I write this, a popular conspiracy blog just posted a series of stories detailing the "lies" that the establishment is using to keep us down, man. Included in the list are vaccinations (bad), Pearl Harbor (inside job), chemtrails (they really are a thing), and the fact that water has memory (suppressed by Big Science, for some reason).[79] It seems to me that these ideas are gaining traction because, while many are increasingly willing to radically question everything, there hasn't been a corresponding willingness to marry that skepticism with any sort of intellectual rigor. It's important to question authority, but questioning isn't enough. One also needs to be able to think.

Since Hopkins's flat Earth ideas involve all the traditional conspiracy tropes (and since much of conspiracy theory has anti-Semitism in its DNA) I had to ask: Does he believe that the Holocaust happened?

"I don't know," Hopkins says. "I wasn't there. Like, a lot of people say, 'Do you believe in the Holocaust?' I wasn't there, I don't know. All I know is that the people that win the wars write the history." He refuses to believe something just because it's taught in school. "I guess I'd have to go over to Germany and do some forensic examination to prove it."

This isn't science, and this isn't skepticism. It's stupidity. While this one guy's crank idea probably isn't too terribly dangerous, it reflects a larger problem of rejecting scientific understanding—not an inability to understand science, but a refusal of its methods and conclusions. How will we possibly hope to thrive and survive, mister, if we're wasting precious time and energy trying to figure out if the Earth is round, if the moon is real, or if the Holocaust even happened?

Everything's up in the air, floating over an obviously, demonstrable, inarguably flat Earth.

The Conspiracy Entrepreneur

(From The Kernel, *November 29, 2015)*

There's no reason you would know who Ben Davidson is, unless you're one of the 250,000 subscribers to his YouTube channel, Suspicious Observers, which boasts of providing "the best open sources of information on Earth." Every morning, all year-round, he posts dispatches from his explorations into "the frontiers of solar and planetary science." In Davidson's world, earthquakes can be predicted by looking at the Earth's electromagnetic output, the sun directly influences things like suicides and crime rates, and water rains down from outer space.

He also holds forth on common conspiracy theories about Agenda 21 (a United Nations sustainability plan often cited as a cover for a coming New World Order), chemtrails (jet aircraft trails said to secretly contain dangerous chemicals), and global warming. In a typical video, he claims that global warming isn't happening, and also that the government is secretly spraying chemicals into the air to stop global warming. And that another ice age is around the corner.[80]

For fans of this material, it isn't the contradictory claims that matter so much as that each of these claims calls the official narrative of anthropogenic climate change into question. Conspiracy theorists eat this stuff up.

Davidson is probably the last person you'd suspect would become a conspiracy entrepreneur. Hailing from Fox Chapel, Pennsylvania, a well-to-do suburb outside Pittsburgh, he studied meteorology in college before receiving a B.A. in economics and then a law degree in 2011. It was around then when the tsunami and subsequent disaster at the Fukushima Daiichi Nuclear Power Plant introduced him to a world of scientific inquiry at odds with the mainstream.

"I became really interested in the Japan earthquake," he tells me, "just because I wanted to understand the raw power of what was going on." This was at a time when pop culture was freaking out over an impending doomsday scheduled for Dec. 21, 2012. You couldn't search for tsunami videos without encountering any number of "alternative" explanations or conspiracy theories about what was really happening in Japan. He found this all fascinating, but the people reporting on this stuff were unreliable. "Wack-jobby," in his words.

He realized that he could apply his investigative skills, picked up in law school and in his day job as a due diligence professional, to the world of conspiracies and government cover-ups. Perhaps, if he worked hard at it, this could become his full-time job. Four years later, he's not only making a living—he's established a haven for hundreds of thousands of people whose outré beliefs make them feel marginalized. In short, he's created a community of believers.

In the spring of 2011, Davidson started posting videos to YouTube. At first, these were pretty basic iMovie creations —collages of found video, soundtracked by hip-hop and with titles like "Intro to Elenin, HAARP, and the 2012 Conspiracy." The news footage and stock photos were interspersed with title cards, on which he editorialized. One typical example:

Do not blame Obama for what you see around you.

This was set in motion long ago, and he is as much a prisoner as you are.

His greatest flaw is his belief that participation in the machine can result in change from within.

Change begins between your ears mate, open your mind.

He'd wake up well before dawn and make videos before going to work. By the fall, he was uploading seven days a week. He says that he doesn't take days off, ever: He's even posted videos on his wedding day and on the morning of his daughter's birth. His fans appreciated the effort, and soon he was gaining hundreds of subscribers a day. In the end of 2013, having reached 100,000 subscribers, he quit his job to peddle conspiracy full time.

These days, he has just shy of a quarter million YouTube subscribers. He also makes money through premium memberships to his website ($29.99/year or $3.99/month), which gives subscribers access to more videos, podcasts, forums, and dossiers. And he recently started organizing conferences where tickets sell for $100 each, or double that to attend the VIP lunch. He's also selling conference videos for the quite reasonable price of $2 per talk, or $18 for the whole set.

"I really miss the paychecks that I got at my old job," he says. We're sitting at a coffee shop in downtown Pittsburgh on a late-September morning. Davidson, who graduated from an area high school in 2003, has the understated authority of a TV weatherman or enthusiastic government official. Talking to him, it's easy to forget that he's only about 30 years old.

Missing paychecks aside, what he does now is more than just a job. It's a service to what he calls "the community," those like-minded people out there who are being lied to, not just by the mainstream media, but by those who are being paid to promote disinformation from within the ranks of the conspiracy movement.

"The majority of the most headline-worthy things in the community," he says, have obviously been "planted" by government shills. "You can see similarities in writing styles.

Sometimes you can go to a bunch of different websites, like *Before It's News*, *Above Top Secret*, and *Godlike Productions*, and [the authors] all have different user names, but they'll all be pushing everyone towards the same thing."

I tell him that I've noticed that myself, how the same story will seem to pop up everywhere at once, and that I'd always attributed it to plagiarism or at least a basic lack of standards. After all, we're talking about internet conspiracy forums.

"It's called controlling the opposition," Davidson corrects me. "I believe the person most responsible for this is Alex Jones." He then schools me on how the Nixon administration would leak negative stories to get them through the news cycle before they had a chance to do real political damage. He's got an analogy brewing. "The idea is to satiate the public's want" for conspiracy news, he says, "while keeping the worst stuff hidden."

I asked Davidson what he brings to his community. He says that he's the "voice of reason. The equilibrium."

Davidson might be the voice of reason, but most people will find his message a little hard to hear. Essentially, he believes that the magnetosphere is weakening, making the Earth susceptible to solar radiation that increasingly wreaks havoc on terrestrial electronics and electrical systems. This is the slow-boil beginning of solar cataclysm, which—followed to its likely conclusion—will mean the end of society as we know it.

Just this past June, he claims, solar storms "nearly sent us back to the stone age." He offers a series of seemingly related news items as proof. There was an aviation radar outage in New Zealand, a digital banking system failure in South Africa, and batteries on board the Solar Impulse 2 experimental aircraft were fried as it flew over the Pacific. Davidson attributes all these events to solar storms, although each has been attributed to other, less apocalyptic explanations. But that's fine with him. While he may currently be at odds with the mainstream media, everybody will catch up to him eventually.

"I'd like to think that I have more humility than to say I'm out on the leading edge of things," he says, "but on a number of topics I've been just a little bit ahead of what the mainstream is willing to accept." By no means is Davidson the first to report on the dangers of extreme weather from space or things like chemtrails and Agenda 21 here on Earth, but he pulls it all together in an even-handed, no-bullshit tone that his fans really appreciate. It's that equilibrium, he says, noting that the truth likely lies "somewhere in between what the craziest people on the Internet are saying, and the straight lies fed by the mainstream media."

In conversation, Davidson uses the word "community" quite a bit. He doesn't have fans, or followers, or customers. And he doesn't trade in conspiracy theories. Rather, he provides vital news and information to the conspiracy community. The borders of this community, as he explains it, are somewhat nebulous. It's concerned with "everything from 9/11 conspiracies to things about GMOs and pollution, to magnetic pole shifts and other natural disasters, and New World Order stuff." This list, of course, is only scratching the surface. There are probably as many theories about how the world *really* works as there are conspiracy theorists. What unites members of this community, according to Davidson, is that they've all experienced what he calls an "awakening." And he includes himself in that group.

I asked Davidson to describe his awakening.

"It's like the realization you go through when you realize why your parents told you what they told you about cannabis," he says. "Imagine that with every aspect of your life. So you have this amazing and fascinating world that's been hidden right in front of your eyes. And it's now open to you. It's more exciting than any plot in a movie or in a book, and it's real. These things are affecting our lives day-to-day and they might really begin to affect our lives significantly. And then you add on top of that the fact that you begin to realize how much you weren't told, and how much you may have been lied to. And you have such a rapid shift from normalcy bias and cognitive dissonance into an awakening that you are now open to anything, because your logical filter has sort of been removed."

And when your logical filter is removed, anything suddenly seems possible. "When you allow yourself to wake up for the first time," he says, "your religion, your childhood fears, anything is open to being taken advantage of by these con men and these doomsayers. A lot of people do go nuts in this community."

As an example of what can go wrong when one experiences an "awakening," he mentions the rampage shooting at the Washington Navy Yard that left 12 people dead in September 2013. "He believed that the government was attacking him with electromagnetic frequencies," Davidson explains. "Most of the people who end up going and shooting [up] movie theaters or malls, these people are into [conspiracy theories]."

According to Davidson, he escaped this all-too-common fate by experiencing a "second awakening," as described in a video that he titled, "I wish I knew this when I 'Woke Up.'" If his first awakening allowed him to pierce the lies told by our government and mainstream media, the second awakening told him that he could only rely on his own investigation if he wanted to know how the world actually works. Awakening, he says, "comes at a price. But it's a price that can be refunded through diligence and hard work, and the application of simple reasoning skills. Just because a terrible realization about the world has changed your way of thinking forever, it does not mean that you should forget everything you've learned about making judgments about people, and checking the facts to see if someone is full of crap."

If you were suddenly awakened to the imminent end of society as you know it, what would you do? I'd be hard-pressed to come up with a better answer than Ben Davidson. He quit his job, raised $60,000 on Kickstarter, bought an RV, outfitted it with a meteor camera, solar telescope, and a radiation detector, and hit the road with his wife and two dogs. For the better part of a year, he traveled the United States and Canada, presenting his scientific findings to anyone who would listen—including local news programs in Joplin, Missouri, and Alberta, Canada. But more rewarding, he says, was connecting with people at the various meet-and-greets they organized along the way.

"People have to be guarded about [conspiracy topics] the majority of their lives," he explains. "They can't go out and strike up a conversation about the New World Order or solar flares with people."

Davidson wasn't just meeting members of an audience he'd only known from the Internet. He was a traveling attractor, bringing together previously isolated members of his tribe. When they came together, many felt at home for the first time. They felt like they were among people who had experienced the same kind of awakening.

"They show up," he says, "and not only does nobody look at them funny or think they're insane, but they're around a bunch of people who are as open and feeling as initially vulnerable as they did. And the connections that people were making, and the amount of fun they had at these events, it was like a 'safe place' to really express these things that are so important to people."

I had an opportunity to see this for myself recently when I attended Davidson's Observing the Frontier conference. For a weekend in October, 120 people from around the region came to Pittsburgh to attend talks on fringe scientific topics, from starwater to fast radio bursts. And more importantly, they had the opportunity to interact with each other—in Q&A sessions, between presentations, and during a VIP lunch rap session with Davidson himself.

My weekend culminated in the conference's Saturday evening happy hour. The atmosphere in the banquet room was relaxed but cheerful. There were several groups huddled together, happily discussing everything from "electric universe" ideas to ancient astronauts to 9/11 conspiracy theories. One particular guy bounced around the room energetically, talking about the connection between the cutting-edge science he was learning here and his own Divine DNA healing techniques. If these people ever felt afraid to discuss their unique take on the world, you'd never know it by watching them here, among their peers.

As the members of his conspiracy community milled around, Davidson stood off to the side of the room by himself, with a drink in his hand and a look of satisfaction on his face. Earlier in the day, I asked him if he was happy with the turnout for his event.

"I'm more happy with online orders" for the conference videos, he replied.

Sure, this is his passion, but it's also his job. And in America, with hard work and the right message, you still can make a living doing what you love. Even if it's crying out in the wilderness about the doom lurking in the heavens.

The Targeted Individuals

(From The Outline, *February 2, 2017)*

It was mid-December, about a week before Christmas, in Phoenix, Arizona. *Phil Drummond* (not his real name) was sitting in a grey Ford Focus, in a Cracker Barrel parking lot. The 23-year-old had a Geiger counter in his pocket, and he was on the phone with a 911 operator.

Operator: Where's the emergency?

Phil: What's going on right now is, there's some issues in regards to a shooting right now. Someone's happened to go ahead and utilize radiological weapons, and there's a conspiracy of terrorism that's occurring right now.

Operator: So, you're seeing shots fired, is that what you're saying?

Phil: No, I'm actually an expert in radiological weapons and psychotronic weapons, and I happen to have a device here that's able to detect that type of weaponry being omitted, and right now this device is going ahead and detecting [these weapons].

Operator: Sir, we have a really poor connection. You need to speak a little slower and talk more directly into your phone.

Phil: Sure, right. There is a radiological weapon that is being fired in the form of radiation, which is a— with that being said, I'm unable to identify a suspect at the moment, but I wanted to give you guys a call to let you know that this type of stuff is occurring, and see if we can get an investigation going forward, or at least I can speak to an officer here.

Phil is a Targeted Individual. He claims that he is being tracked and tormented by a loose network of anonymous agents wielding exotic, top secret weaponry. I repeatedly asked him for some sort of evidence of his harassment, without any luck. Then, just before Christmas, Phil sent me the audio recording of his encounter with the Phoenix Police Department.

There was a time when this might have seemed funny. But that was before conspiracy theory was weaponized to help win elections, before the whole world seemed to lose its collective mind. After Edgar Maddison Welch stormed Comet Ping Pong with an AR-15, motivated by tales of a child-sex ring spun in troll breeding grounds like 4chan, I wasn't feeling so great writing about conspiracy theorists like Phil anymore. Then I learned that both Baton Rouge cop-killer Gavin Long and the FSU shooter Myron May were self-described Targeted Individuals.

Soon after making the 911 call, Phil found himself knees-down on the pavement, hands behind his back, towered over by a cop wielding an AR-15.

After Phil was moved to the back seat of a police car, there was maybe 20 minutes' worth of near-silence on the recording, punctuated occasionally by weird electronic bleeps and buzzes and overheard snippets of the cop radio.

In the midst of all this, Phil let out a loud, weary breath. The kind of breath that sounded like, How the hell did I get myself into this?

Like Phil, *Brian Tanner* (also not his real name) is a Targeted Individual—a victim of "gang stalking," or surveillance and harassment at the hands of the government or private security firms. This is an internet subculture of people who believe that they're being hounded by a secret police force that most of us don't even agree exists.

For a number of years, Brian said, he was a security professional in the California offices of a large multinational corporation. At first, things went pretty well for him—until a minor disagreement with his boss sent everything spiraling out of control. Soon, he found himself the target of workplace bullying, or "mobbing."

It took some time for Brian to even realize that he was being harassed, but eventually it was evident that he was being spied on at his home as well as at work. For example, Brian might have a conversation with his girlfriend after hours, then hear the same conversation at work the next day. "People [at work] would be told things to say," he said. "I don't know if they even knew themselves what they were always specifically referencing, but just things that made it clear that I was being watched very closely at my residence."

Brian is convinced that his landlord, an "older, super-conservative white dude who's got friends who are cops," was conducting "pretty high-tech surveillance" and coordinating with his tormentors in the office. "And so then, it was just like pure hell."

Eventually Brian lost his job, his apartment, and his girlfriend. These days, he works in a production facility, doing "low-level logistics and warehouse work," while suffering what he described as persistent, high-tech harassment.

According to Brian, the American security apparatus (including the intelligence community, all levels of law enforcement, and private spooks like Stratfor and HBGary) is more vast, more out-of-control than even Julian Assange would suspect. The result of having so many people running around with surveillance tools and law enforcement connections is that America is a de facto surveillance state, where we're all victims of decentralized, lone wolf Stasi. Most of us just haven't realized it yet.

As for Brian, all he really knows is that he feels persecuted and that this persecution defies reasonable expectation. Unable to document hard evidence of his harassment, he assembled a theory to explain what might be happening to him.

"I personally think that there are different people," he said, "different groups who use these same tactics." According to Brian, all sorts of groups have the mandate (and the technology, and the budget) to target anyone who pisses them off. Many of these people are "ex-cops or former agents. They know these tactics. I don't think there's a single entity that coordinates federally all this stuff that's going on."

So far, however implausible Brian's story may seem, it certainly is possible. That is, it's all within the realm of material possibility. How about the more exotic stuff, the psychotronic weapons that Phil reported? I wondered if Brian had been targeted by anything like that.

"It's called V2K [voice-to-skull] technology," Brian explained, "which is where you electronically generate a sound, but the sound essentially can only be heard by the person that you're pointing the device at."

Brian has felt the effects of V2K firsthand.

"It's not a painful thing," he continued, "it's not like you're being zapped, but you just hear a noise. But the noise, it doesn't sound — you can tell when you hear it, it doesn't sound like it's external. You hear it as a sound, it has a clear property, like a noise or a sound, but it doesn't sound like it's coming from around you. It's hard to describe, but it's real. It's totally real."

This isn't something that Brian really wants to talk about.

"It's impossible to describe this," he said, "without having it go through your mind that this is going to sound textbook crazy. Because it's like okay, so you hear voices."

It's classified technology, he explained, the news of which only escapes the Pentagon black box in dribs and drabs. "It's one of those things where people know that it exists, but there's no sort of official public discussion about [it]. It's classified, but it's known. It's in that realm, and I can tell you from experience that it's real."

QuWave is a New Jersey-based online retailer of gadgets designed to protect you from the deleterious effects of electromagnetic radiation. These things are supposed to produce "scalar waves" using "Schumann resonance," both concepts that are very popular in the pseudoscientific community. Among QuWave's product line is the USB Harmonizer, a $159 dongle that somehow turns anything with a USB port into "a radiating source of stabilizing healthy energy." The company also sells something called Defender, which "uses Scalar Waves and Solfeggio Energies to protect effected [sic] individuals from electronic harassment, EMF, psychotronic, spiritual, and psychic attacks."

I called QuWave with a concocted story about a roommate who was hearing voices and feeling "out of it" — as if drugged or being subjected to psychotronic weaponry. I also said that I was feeling pretty "anxious and out of it" myself lately (you'd be too, if your roommate was hearing voices). I left a message with an operator, and a product specialist named Amy returned my call in a matter of minutes.

"Usually the V2K is electronic harassment," she explained. "That's going to be using frequencies directed at your roommate, probably. They use pulses to make you hear voices. So what our product does is it emits a high-frequency scalar wave that scrambles those frequencies that are being directed at them, so that they can't get to them, and it should stop the voices."

She told me that it seemed like the number of Targeted Individuals has been increasing over the four years or so that she'd been with the company. "It's very similar obviously to some mental illness, so I think we have some customers who aren't sure what's going on, but they don't want to think it's mental illness. Basically, the biggest difference between mental illness and being electronically harassed is, if you have a mental illness it usually shows up throughout your life. Whereas, electronic harassment usually starts out of nowhere, or from specific events. Talking to customers, whistleblowers a lot of the time it will happen to them, or if somebody has a big lawsuit against the city or state or a large company."

Amy said she knew nothing about any of this before she was hired. "But now I'm a product specialist, and now I know too much!" she laughed.

"This type of technology came out a long time ago, in the 1940s and 1950s," she explained, "and it was used by the CIA during war as human experiments. It's actually, if you Google 'MK-ULTRA,' they used this type of technology. It's supposed to be illegal, it was supposed to be shut down, but clearly that hasn't happened. Not completely, anyways."

But Amy admitted that the Personal Defender (list price: $297) wasn't for everybody.

"I've even got calls," she said, "being yelled at by people's caretakers or parents or whatever, because they know that their child does have a mental illness, and they ordered the product. I assure them that if that's the case then obviously the product's not going to work, and they can send it back."

Of course, V2K has not been proven to exist, so there's little chance that a USB dongle will stop the voices in your head, regardless of the cause. Fortunately, QuWave products include a money-back guarantee.

The intersection of science and national security is indeed a very weird place. If you believe the Targeted Individuals, it's a place where governments and corporations collaborate to develop high-tech super-weapons and surveillance gear that works almost as if by magic. The more unscrupulous contractors, this theory goes, even take these inventions out of the laboratory, where they're tested on innocent civilians.

At least, this is the premise of a book called *Chameleo: A Strange But True Story of Invisible Spies, Heroin Addiction, and Homeland Security* by Robert Guffey. *Chameleo* is the story of *Dion*, a pseudonymous friend of Guffey's with a fondness for "speed and meth and heroin and everything in between." In the book, which is published as nonfiction, Dion ends up in jail for possession of stolen goods—including 25 pairs of night-vision goggles and a laptop taken from the Department of Defense by an AWOL Marine who was crashing on Dion's couch. This was in the early days of the global War on Terror, and Dion's treatment at the hands of his jailers is described as resembling something out of Abu Ghraib. Dion was never charged with the crime.

If you believe Guffey, Dion's run-in with the law put him on a "list" of some sort. Soon after his release, Dion realized he was being followed; at first, by people in unmarked police cars. But eventually, he came to realize that "invisible midgets" (his words, not mine) were running amok in his apartment.

The book gets its title from "Chameleo," the commercial name for an as-yet-unrealized invisibility technology patented in the early 1990s by an engineer living in Costa Mesa, California, named Richard Schowengerdt.

"Most of my career has been with the military," Schowengerdt told me recently. "Department of Defense. I have about 10 years of aerospace experience." According to an article by Guffey in the now-defunct *UFO Magazine*, Schowengerdt's work over the last five years has included a number of innovations in the field of electromagnetics—including development of the first digital voltmeters, a concept for closed-loop testing of guided missiles, and work on the EA-18G Growler combat aircraft.[81]

"I did some experimentation" with Chameleo in the lab, Schowengerdt told me over the phone, "but we don't have a working mock-up that we can show you."

That said, he's pretty sure the Army has developed a working model. "I've seen pictures of it, demos of it" online. "It's pretty good, you know. There are little imperfections there, but it's working."

I'm pretty sure that the demos he refers to are actually green screen mock-ups that were featured on a CNN segment a few years back, but I let it drop. I was more interested in hearing his impression of Dion. So I asked Schowengerdt, was somebody using Dion to test Chameleo?

"I believe so, yeah," he replied. "He was probably the first."

I then asked if Dion's story aligned with what he described in his patent.

"Yes, pretty much," he said. "All they'd done to him was done at night, and apparently they went into his house and moved things around, according to him. He was under some suspicion because he was a drug addict, but he was not a drug addict at that particular time. So there's some credibility to what he says."

"Psychotronics" is a word coined by a Soviet-era Czech scientist to replace the the scientifically discredited term "parapsychology." The term "psychotronic weapons" has been adopted by conspiracy theorists to mean any sort of weapon that uses things like extremely low frequency (ELF) waves to control a victim's emotions or make them hear voices.

According to Jonathan D. Moreno, a professor of medical ethics at the University of Pennsylvania and author of *Mind Wars: Brain Science and the Military in the 21st Century*, there simply isn't any proof that psychotronic weapons have been developed, or that they could even work. He stops short of saying that psychotronic weapons don't exist, pointing out helpfully that you can't prove a negative.

"This is like a baby boomer conspiracy theory, you know?" he said. "This is an old idea. When I was a kid we were excited about lasers and all they could do, and some of the old science fiction movies messed around with this stuff. It's getting old-fashioned." With all that's in the news these days, from escalating nuclear tensions to the growth of far-right politics, psychotronic weapons are simply "not sexy anymore, even as a fantasy," let alone as the subject of military research.

But all this is of little comfort to Phil Drummond, whose life has been steadily falling apart over the last few years. He's had multiple scrapes with the law, including a pot bust and some sort of physical altercation with his stepdad. And there was a cross-country road trip, during which he said he was bombarded by radiation. As proof of this last point, he sent me video of a Geiger counter registering what appeared to be dangerously high radiation levels, but I couldn't really say what that actually demonstrated.

Phil insisted that he has meticulous documentation of his harassment, but aside from the one video, he was unwilling (or unable) to produce any of it for me. My efforts to get some sort of concrete evidence out of him eventually led to a terse email exchange.

"Perhaps after its [sic] ensured that we both share the same values for journalism," Phil wrote, "I will present to you everything I have in bulk. Its [sic] nothing personal, its [sic] just that proof of what some people call 'mind control' can be a little hard to handle."

And that was the last that I heard from the guy until the week before Christmas, when he emailed me the audio recordings of his run-in with the Phoenix Police Department. This is an example of "what happens when you report radiological weapons (a component of gang stalking) to law enforcement," he wrote. "You get assault rifles drawn on you with the police not having a clue as to what they're even pointing guns for. The conversation that occurs with the last cop is the best."

The "last cop" that Phil referred to is a member of the department's Crisis Intervention Squad (CIS), also known as the "mental health squad." The CIS was called in after first responders determined that Phil wasn't actually threatening the city of Phoenix with a weapon of mass destruction, even if it sounded like he was to the 911 operator.

The CIS officer politely but firmly told Phil that his claims seemed "very, very far-fetched. Because you have no proof, and no real idea of who's doing this to you." He then offered his business card, which Phil took. Then he suggested a mental health evaluation, which Phil politely declined.

After hearing the tape, I was concerned for Phil's well-being. I wondered if this brush with law enforcement could be some sort of escalation, and if I should be worried. I decided to give him a call and check in. But first, I took a look at his Facebook page. The latest update was from Christmas Eve. In the post, he spoke about fighting back against government mind control, and using his "blue steel" to do so.

"The moment when you realize you've gotta use your blue steel to fight back," it said. "#mindcontrol"

This didn't seem very good.

"Blue steel" or "bluing" can refer to a technique for protecting the metal finish of a firearm. Perhaps the status update was referencing "Blue Steel" by MOP ("Say what, say what, say what? / I'm packin blue steel / Plow! I'm shootin muthafuckas in the belly"). Was Phil announcing his intention to shoot someone? Concerned, I gave him a call.

"Are you safe right now?" I asked, after an initial greeting. "I just noticed a Facebook post where you mentioned mind control and 'blue steel,' so I just wanted to make sure you're okay."

"Yeah," he replied, in his sort of stilted manner of speaking. Imagine Dan Aykroyd's Conehead voice but an octave lower and with more weird vocal tics. "In regards to that post, it was posted with a humorous intent."

I asked him if he had a gun, if I should be worried.

"I'm not too sure where you go ahead and get as to where you need to be concerned about me, Joseph. That was you know, a jokative post. Have you ever seen *Zoolander*?"

No, I haven't. If I had, I would know that "blue steel" has another, less ominous meaning.

For some reason, Phil seemed to be in a hurry to get off the phone.

Everyone (well, almost everyone) I talked to while writing this story came across as credible, as very normal. Targeted Individuals are obviously experiencing something highly traumatic and anxiety-inducing, something they're at a loss to adequately understand. Otherwise, they all tend to be pretty unremarkable. That is, you probably wouldn't be able to pick one out in a lineup. If anything, the people I spoke with seemed a little smarter than the average.

Ian Gold, a professor of philosophy and psychiatry at McGill University and co-author of the book *Suspicious Minds: How Culture Shapes Madness*, told me that I shouldn't be surprised that I would find delusional beliefs in otherwise normal-seeming individuals. "Delusions are symptoms," he said, "not illnesses in their own right." Unless someone has a mental illness that manifests other, more extreme behavior, someone with "a relatively isolated island of delusional thought" is going to otherwise appear "perfectly normal."

In fact, Gold explained, "lots of people who are delusional never come to the attention of psychiatrists."

Now, I have no desire to diagnose anybody, even if I could. The most I'm willing to say about any of the individual claims here is that I'm not convinced that the institutional "gang stalking," the phenomenon that Brian and others have described, is actually happening. There very well could be truth to some of the claims made by Targeted Individuals, but I just don't believe that the surveillance state works in the way that they described.

But it's hard to entirely dismiss the Targeted Individuals—probably because the framework for their theoretical dystopia conforms so closely to that of the currently existing dystopia that's been unveiled by whistleblowers and investigative journalists over the last several years. When Edward Snowden's revelations were made public in 2013, the reaction in the Targeted Individual community must have been little more than a wary "told you so." And most recently, a raft of FBI documents uncovered by *The Intercept* revealed how the federal law enforcement agency (using the war on terrorism as a pretext) dismantled reforms enacted after the COINTELPRO disclosures of the 1970s.[82]

"If you're a psychiatrist," Gold said, "and someone comes into your office and says, 'Oh, I've been kidnapped by the NSA and they put a microphone in my tooth,'" that person is probably delusional. "But if another patient comes in and says, 'People across America are being kidnapped by the NSA and microphones are being inserted into their teeth,'" that's not a delusion. It's a conspiracy theory.

The idea that people with unrealistic or unreasonable ideas (read: conspiracy theorists) can be almost functionally identical to people with a mental disorder gives me considerable pause. If this is the case, a population solely informed by fake news, pseudoscience, and pseudohistory would be almost indistinguishable from a population of psychotics. Psychotics suffer from a disorder that causes them to lose contact with reality. And it is now painfully obvious that flooding social media with "fake news" can have the impact of severing non-psychotics from reality just as severely. Of course, reality does tend to reassert itself eventually, if seldom in time to prevent large-scale Trump voter remorse.

The percentage of the population with delusional disorder is quite low, while the percentage of the population that can't tell a real news story from *The Onion* (or Fox News) only seems to be growing. If this continues, a generation fed on a steady diet of internet bullshit is going to make the current community of Targeted Individuals seem rather quaint and charming.

The world may very well be going crazy, whether or not it has a diagnosable disorder.

EPILOGUE

(An abridged version of this story appeared in Counterpunch *on November 16, 2018)*

> "I have never had any special fear of Foreigners, myself, but I recognize a nationwide nervous breakdown when I see one. It is embarrassing, for openers, and it sucks."
> — Hunter S. Thompson, *Kingdom of Fear*

The reporter on TV has just detailed his "chilling" encounter with the killer in a Pittsburgh courtroom. I was present in the courtroom as well, and I have no idea what the hell he is talking about.

It was the initial court appearance of Robert D. Bowers, the individual who killed 11 and wounded several others at the Tree of Life synagogue in Pittsburgh on Saturday, October 27, 2018.[83] Bowers, who received 29 federal and 36 state charges, was pushed into the courtroom in a wheelchair. With his gray sweatpants, blue sweatshirt, dollar store black plastic slippers and thinning hair, he could be any problem drinker at a local Pittsburgh bar; except that his arms and legs were shackled to his wheelchair. He looked around the courtroom as he entered, but nothing appeared to register for him. It's not that he wasn't alert—just that he was possibly a bit of a "dull blade," if you know what I mean; certainly, he was in over his head. When asked if he would waive his right to bail, he said, simply, "yes." When asked if he needed a public defender, he said, "yes." That was about the extent of the hearing, although to hear David Begnaud of CBSN relay the hearing to his TV audience, the killer's appearance was "chilling," something out of a horror film (or an episode of *Law and Order: Special Victims Unit*).*

But what do I know? Unlike the credentialed journalists, I had to hand my smartphone over to security before entering the court. I'm a second-class media citizen and certainly not a trusted name in TV news. Maybe the guy from New York (is he from New York? aren't they all from New York?) is right, and the courtroom scene actually

* My read of the situation is corroborated by Ari Mahler, the Jewish nurse who treated Bowers two days earlier. "I didn't see evil when I looked into Robert Bowers' eyes," he wrote on Facebook. "All I saw was a clear lack of depth, intelligence, and palpable amounts of confusion." (He later amended this to say: "I didn't see evil when I looked into Robert Bower's eyes. I saw something else. I can't go into details [sic] of our interactions because of HIPAA.") Martin Pengelly, "Nurse who treated Pittsburgh shooter: 'I'm sure he had no idea I was Jewish,'" *The Guardian*, November 4, 2018. http://archive.fo/aQrmL

was as dramatic as he conveyed on television. I mean, I'm not comfortable saying that Bernaud is full of shit. Just that, you know, there are a few ways to look at this.

Perhaps he wanted to perceive evil in the presence of Bowers, because at least that would go some way towards explaining how such a tragedy might have happened. Because the reality of the situation is that Bowers didn't live in a white nationalist compound somewhere in remote Idaho wilderness—he lived in a crappy apartment in the same building as a plumbing and heating company, in a neighborhood lined with modest single-story brick houses. Sitting on the pavement outside his apartment door was a rusted out barbecue smoker with an upturned Dunkin' Donuts coffee cup on the top; an empty bottle of Bud Light was on the ground between the smoker and the front door. The building was near an old coal patch where, according to a neighbor named Terrance Holleran, "there's been a couple homicides" in the last few years. He didn't know Bowers; none of his neighbors seemed to. In Holleran's words, it "is just unfortunate that this asshole chose to live here."

The more we learn about Bowers, the less remarkable he becomes. He was a long-haul truck driver, friendly enough to the neighbors but generally kept to himself.[84] It was only online where he felt free to unleash his inner raving lunatic. Before the attack, he posted the following on his social media account (he was a verified user of Gab, the Twitter of the extreme right): "HIAS [the refugee aid nonprofit] likes to bring invaders in that kill our people. I can't sit by and watch my people get slaughtered. Screw your optics, I'm going in."[85]

"Screw your optics" refers to a lover's quarrel among the far-right over "optics," or whether they should worry about how crazy they appear to people outside the movement. And the invasion he referred to is the current, Donald Trump-fueled hysteria about an alleged, imminent invasion of brown people on our southern border.

Bowers didn't care whether or not he appeared crazy. And he was unquestionably deranged: he entered a house of worship and when he came face-to-face with some of the sweetest, most harmless looking senior citizens you could imagine, he pulled the trigger. He considered murdering them the same way that most of us consider setting a mouse trap; that is, he doesn't seem to have given it any thought at all. Of course, that's the most troubling part of all this. What sort of ugly mchanism was at work here?

Bowers' actions were certainly evil, so perhaps it is understandable that we'd want him to act evil or seem evil in court. I looked, but I just didn't see it. The Robert D. Bowers who committed what is said to be the deadliest anti-Semitic attack in American history[86] was much different than the guy the U.S. Marshals wheeled out in front of me.

According to the criminal complaint:

> During the course of his deadly assault on people at the Synagogue, and simultaneously with his gunfight with responding officers, BOWERS made statements evincing an animus towards people of

the Jewish faith. For example, BOWERS commented to one law enforcement officer, in substance, "they're committing genocide to my people. I just want to kill Jews." BOWERS repeated comments regarding genocide, his desire to kill Jewish people, and that Jewish people needed to die.[87]

Until the shooting, Bowers had "moved through the Pittsburgh area . . . leaving relatively little impression," according to the *Pittsburgh Post Gazette*.[88] But violence had been lying just under the surface for quite some time.

"Much of Bowers' online profile resembles those of countless other extremist users," according to a Southern Poverty Law Center analysis of the shooter's social media. "As with other alt-right killers, it's likely that Bowers was radicalized entirely online." His social media activity revolved around several common obsessions of the racist right. He feared "white genocide," an anti-Semitic conspiracy theory which holds that everything from immigration and multiculturalism to low birth rates and abortion are being promoted by the "globalists" (that's an anti-Semitic code word for "Jews") to drive the white race to extinction. In Bowers' virtual reality, the white men have no power—undoubtedly resonant to a white man who seemed to have little in his own life worth living for—while George Soros (another anti-Semitic code word for "Jews") is personally overseeing the extinction of the white race. [89]

"Lone wolf terror" (sometimes called "leaderless resistance") describes terrorist attacks conducted by a single person, or perhaps a very small, unaffiliated group. According to terrorism expert George Michael, the author of *Lone Wolf Terror and the Rise of Leaderless Resistance*, it is commonly understood among right-wing populists that "they are part of a relatively small and marginalized movement," and that to take up arms "would almost certainly lead to organizational suicide," not to mention actual suicide. This has led to the strategy, favored by the more conservative members of the right-wing populist movement, to concentrate on winning the masses over through propaganda.[90]

The more extreme elements of right-wing populism, not willing to abandon armed struggle, have encouraged "lone wolves" to pick up arms. The idea is that individuals like Bowers and MAGA mail bomber Cesar Sayoc are the vanguard of a new movement that's paving the way for a right-wing takeover of the United States. Now, this might be the case—but probably not in the way that the extremists like to imagine.

"Under specific conditions," writes journalist and activist Chip Berlet, "virulent demonization and scapegoating can—and does—create milieus in which the potential for violence is increased." While you can't predict which individual will turn to violence, you can pretty much guarantee that someone will, "upon hearing the rhetoric of clear or coded incitement," strike out at the perceived enemy.[91]

Right-wing populism is a continuum. The extreme right (which Berlet also refers to as "the ultra-right") is the revolutionary arm of right-wing populism in America. This includes the Klan, neo-Nazis, Aryan Nations, and anyone willing to pick up a gun or a baseball bat or make a pipe bomb for the struggle. Among the more conservative elements of right-wing populism are "reformist political movements." These include the Republican Party, Fox News, and conservative think tanks. In between these two poles—the revolutionaries and the reformers—are the dissidents. This includes patriot and militia groups, right-wing talk radio, tea partiers, and anti-Semitic conspiracy theorists.[92] There is a lot of movement along this continuum: people might be drawn into right-wing talk radio, for instance, which becomes a conduit to a more extreme right-wing ideology.

Quite possibly, this is what happened to Robert Bowers. According to the *Pittsburgh Post-Gazette*, Bowers is believed to have once been the webmaster or audio archivist (or both) for local right-wing talk show host—and Rush Limbaugh protege—Jim Quinn.[93] (To give you an idea of the kind of right-wing kook Jim Quinn is, his show is available via live stream from the warroom.com website. His current billboards, as seen around the city, feature his geriatric mug lighting a cigar with a lighter shaped like an assault rifle.)

Where does the current president factor into all this? Most of us are quick to assume that Bowers' fit of violence must be somehow connected to Trump—even if Bowers considered Trump to be a part of the problem, a "globalist," and therefore at least partially responsible for the "kike invasion."[94]

In a recent talk, Berlet described how right-wing groups are often tools of the elites;* as a result, right-wing populist groups often receive encouragement (and funding) from those in power. The elites aren't trying to reform the system, of course; they're using the populist desire for reform to get one up on their political rivals.

"Cynical politicians emerge using populist-sounding rhetoric to mobilize the angry social movement into a political constituency," according to Berlet. In the end, the winner is "a selected group within the society who are seeking to defend . . . unfair power and privilege."

Ultimately, right-wing populism is a tool that is used by cynical elites for their own political advantage. However, right-wing rage is not something that can be controlled. Once unleashed, it will go wherever it goes; Trumpian hate speech one day becomes anti-Semitic violence the next.

---

* To be clear, we're not using the word "elites" in the paranoid conspiracist's sense. This comes from American sociologist C. Wright Mills, whose 1956 book *The Power Elite* examined the "small group of wealthy and powerful individuals [who control] America's dominant institutions (i.e., political, economic and military)." http://archive.fo/DZMhQ

Shortly after the Tree of Life shooting, Pennsylvania Governor Tom Wolf and Pittsburgh Public Safety Director Wendell Hissrich walked over to the corner of Murray Avenue and Northumberland Street where the press was awaiting their statement. I don't know how it came across on television, but the governor, having just seen the the bloody aftermath of the massacre, was visibly shaken, speaking so softly that he could hardly be heard a few feet away. And Hissrich, a 25-year veteran of the FBI, was visibly upset. Indeed, it seemed as if he might start weeping at any moment. As the press conference commenced, numerous first responders filed past—many of which, aside from patches that said POLICE or CIRT, were nearly indistinguishable from soldiers fighting in Iraq or Afghanistan.

Earlier in this book, I explained the recovered memory movement as "conspiracy theory practices medicine." The Comet Ping Pong shooting was cited as an example of what happens when conspiracy theory picks up a gun. The Tree of Life synagogue shooting is another, much more horrifying, example of the latter.

Very few conspiracy theorists (self-identified or otherwise) are violent antisemites, although virtually all antisemites are conspiracy theorists. And conspiracy theory is one of the more effective tools in the despot's toolbox. "Whether it's in Hitler's Germany, Assad's Syria, or contemporary Turkey," writes Oxford Sociology fellow Turkay Salim Nefes, "the official use of conspiracy rhetoric is a powerful political tool." We should probably add the contemporary United States to the list. In all the examples listed above, conspiracy theories have been "used entirely rationally to justify political views" that otherwise wouldn't even be considered by rational people.[95] The Tree of Life killer believed that he was striking out at those who are behind the invasion of America. That America is being invaded is precisely what the Trump administration wants us to believe—why else is the president mobilizing up to 15,000 troops to the southern border?[96] The nonexistent refugee "invasion" is simply another crackpot conspiracy theory that's being championed by the Republican party and right-wing media outlets.

Before there even was an "official narrative" of the Tree of Life shooting, members of the online conspiracy community were poking holes in it. On *The Memory Hole Blog*, the website of former Florida Atlantic University professor (and Boston Marathon Bombing Truther) James Tracy, an analysis[97] was posted which concluded that the massacre was a hoax, that the alleged victims are what is known as "crisis actors."* Chief among the items supporting this theory was the fact that, in the analyst's opinion, the

* In real life, a crisis actor is someone used to portray the victim of a terrorist attack or natural disaster during training exercises. In conspiracy-world, a crisis actor is a person who pretends to be a victim during fake terrorist attacks, like Sandy Hook or the Boston Marathon bombing.

bystanders they saw on TV didn't seem to be upset enough. (In fact, the shooting victims were sequestered until they could be interviewed by police, so the bystanders that they saw were mostly reporters and a few curious neighbors.) One cited example of inappropriate levity was a joke that Chuck Diamond, former Rabbi of the Tree of Life, made during an interview.

The gunman had entered the synagogue soon after it opened its doors on Saturday morning.

"Jews come late to services," Diamond said. "So for a lot of people, that's probably a good thing."

The author of the analysis can't imagine that someone would crack a joke during a crisis. Or she finds it easier to believe that the government would create a fake terrorist incident, including 11 faked deaths, absent of any supporting evidence.

Also suspicious was the fact that a GoFundMe campaign for victims of the shooting has surpassed the half-million dollar mark ("Mass shootings are . . . a growth industry," according to the author). Ultimately, the conspiracy theorists claim that the Pittsburgh shooting was staged to give Congress an excuse to pass gun control legislation, and make a few people rich in the process. Which begs the question: if after countless "false flag" terror attacks the American public hasn't yet been disarmed, wouldn't the conspirators try something else?

Of course, the answer to this question is that there is no conspiracy; or, perhaps, that there are many conspiracies, many factions watching the American empire fall apart,[*] many factions jockeying for position in the great crack-up. Some of which have no problem filling people's heads with violent rhetoric, if that's what it takes to amass political power.

There was once a strong leftist current in conspiracy theory culture. The rightward shift came, according to Mark Jacobson, when right-wing populists started smoking pot.[**]

"Conspiracy was about connecting dots that seemed irrationally arrayed," Jacobson writes in *Pale Horse Rider*. "Religion did it one way, but pot did it another [way]." And now that more states are legalizing cannabis, "one could only expect more paranoid thinking in the future."[98]

I don't know if I fully buy the cannabis-conspiracy connection—it seems a little too cute to be true—but I would certainly agree that these days conspiracy theory is much more of a right-wing game. Conspiracy theories are too easily weaponized to not be part of the fascist's arsenal.

* "The demise of the United States as the preeminent global power could come far more quickly than anyone imagines. Despite the aura of omnipotence empires often project, most are surprisingly fragile … When their revenues shrink, empires become brittle." Alfred W. McCoy, *In the Shadows of the American Century*, pg. 227

** Jacobson credits this insight to Paul Krassner, journalist and editor of *The Realist*. Krassner places the blame for right-wing conspiracy culture squarely at the feet of the Marshall Tucker Band.

"This is sociology 101," says Chip Berlet. "If a popular leader, if they're very high-up—it doesn't matter if they're political or they're religious, or a movement leader— basically alleges that some group of people is conspiring against the common good and they sort of harp on that for some time, it's only a matter of time before people get killed."[99] This could not be any more clear than in these two examples from the same week: both Cesar Sayoc's hit list[100] and Robert Bowers' "globalist" victims were originally targets of Donald Trump's rhetoric.

Articles and blog posts explaining the psychological basis of conspiracy theory beliefs are perennial news items. They usually have clever titles like "Why Do People Believe in Conspiracy Theories?"[101] People are susceptible to cognitive biases[102] and teleological thinking,[103] the argument goes, both of which cause them to see meaningful patterns where none exist. In these stories, the conspiracy theorist is presented as the cognitively impaired *other*: "You're not a kook, not like those *other* weirdos," the authors seem to be saying. "We've proven it. With science."

While it is true that conspiracy theory beliefs are a result of quirks in human cognition, there are also social causes that need to be factored in. Conspiracism is largely the worldview of the powerless.[104] It expands to fill the vacuum left by a loss of power (or historical lack of power). But in the hands of a savvy political operator, conspiracy theory is just another method of control.

In this fragmented age, leaderless "lone wolf" resistance is particularly trenchant. All it requires is a weapon and an imbalanced mind—no connection with another human being is necessary, besides maybe the false sense of community offered by a Gab account. Likewise, in a time when the traditional American institutions are no longer trusted,[105] conspiracism is a tailor-made philosophy.

This is the dark side of conspiracy culture, the conspiracy-within-the-conspiracy: while conspiracy theorists may believe they are empowered by their idiosyncratic beliefs, conspiracism is actually a measure of their powerlessness, a vehicle for their exploitation.

On Tuesday, three days after the massacre, the funerals began. David and Cecil Rosenthal (ages 54 and 59 respectively) were Bowers' youngest victims. The brothers were roommates at a residential facility for adults with developmental disabilities, and never missed a Saturday at Tree of Life. I have never met David, but Cecil was my buddy—for the better part of a year, we would wait at the same bus stop each morning. He would always say hello, and once he even told me that I had "pretty hair." (That was the first time I suspected that he was maybe an adult with developmental disabilities.)

The service was held at the Rodef Shalom Congregation. The brothers' caskets, closed, were arranged front and center. By the time their brother-in-law, Michael Hirt, told us an anecdote about the brothers' yearly trip to the flea market (Cecil would always buy a new calendar and a watch, while David invariably picked out a bottle of cologne and mirrored *CHiPs*-style sunglasses) everybody in the room was on the verge of tears.

I wrote the following in my notebook: "*Jesus Christ, this is heartbreaking.*"

The mourning ritual focused on the victims. Bowers' name didn't come up once, and aside from an argument over gun control between two old ladies sitting next to me in the balcony, neither did politics. Despite the presence of the mayor and several Pittsburgh Steelers, the focus stayed solely on the victims, just as it should have.

On this same day, the president was scheduled to visit the crime scene. It has been reported that the he had displayed rare flashes of humanity in the period following the attacks, but for the most part these were overshadowed by all-too-familiar Trumpisms.

Pittsburgh Mayor Bill Peduto said that he received a call from the president on the morning of the shooting. The president offered his condolences, then quickly started talking about the death penalty. "I'm literally standing two blocks from 11 bodies right now," Peduto told *The Washington Post*. "Really?" The death penalty would do nothing for the survivors, and it wouldn't bring back the dead—this was simply partisan bullshit coming at the most inappropriate time. "I ended the conversation pretty quickly after that."[106]

Not long after that phone call Trump was in the news, talking up the death penalty and the need for armed guards in synagogues—a "Second Amendment solution" to right-wing violence that placed the blame on the Jews who dared practice their religion unarmed.[107]

Hours after David and Cecil's funeral, I was standing at the police checkpoint near the Tree of Life. On my side of the street there were an estimated 2,000-plus protesters with signs that said things like "Denounce White Nationalism" and "Nazi Trump Fuck Off!" Two blocks away, the president and his wife placed rocks on a memorial dedicated to the eleven victims, the White House's idea of an appropriately understated, religiously neutral ritual. In between us and them, a small group of riot cops stood on alert. They were lined up behind a dump truck that had been positioned to block the street, should the protestors get any ideas. The White House had invited a number of politicians to join them on the trip, "including the Senate and House Republican majority leaders, their Democratic counterparts [and] Mayor Bill Peduto." All of those invited, sensing a political minefield, wisely declined.[108]

The slow, solemn march of the protest through Squirrel Hill was a ritual itself—a civic ritual performed by and for a population who were angry and frightened. The truth, which perhaps they'd been able to avoid thinking about thus far in this season of bloodshed, could no longer be ignored: our Conspiracy-Theorist-in-Chief thinks nothing of using violent rhetoric and outright lies to gain and to keep power. And this violent rhetoric inevitably leads to physical violence. This is all straight from the despot's playbook.

Robert Bowers, sad and violent and isolated, his worst impulses encouraged by forces he couldn't quite understand, marks the end result of a particularly vile process. He may be locked up, awaiting trial, but his accomplices are many and they're unlikely to pay for their crimes anytime soon.

PITTSBURGH, PA
NOVEMBER 2018

ACKNOWLEDGEMENTS

Thank you to all the people who've read various versions of this book and offered feedback and/or encouragement. This includes, in no particular order: Nathan Kukulski, Holly Hickling, Cathy Clark Hickling, Becky Davenport, Alexander Zaitchik, Pearse Redmond, and Yasha Levine.

Thanks also to my father, who accompanied me on my trip to Chicago, and Matt Stroud, who drove me to Comet Ping Pong. And Chuck Ochelli, who had me on his radio show to discuss the Pittsburgh shooting. A great deal of this book's epilogue was fleshed out on his show that night.

Jesse Hicks served as my editor for a couple of the stories in this book, and they are much better for his input.

This book wouldn't exist if Evan Anderson hadn't told me about the ISST-D in the first place. I'd also like to thank Lucien Greaves and Sarah Ponto Rivera for being especially helpful and supportive of my reporting on the group.

Last but not least, thank you to everyone I interviewed for this book. I am indebted to each and every one of you.

SELECTED SOURCES

BOOKS

H.P. Albarelli, *A Terrible Mistake: The Murder of Frank Olson and the CIA's Secret Cold War Experiments*, Walterville, OR: Trine Day, 2009

American Psychiatric Association, *Diagnostic and Statistical Manual of Mental Disorders, Fourth Edition* fourth printing *(DSM-IV)*, Washington, D.C.: American Psychiatric Association, 1995

William Sims Bainbridge, *Satan's Power: A Deviant Psychotherapy Cult*, Berkeley: University of California Press, 1978

Michael Barkun, *A Culture of Conspiracy: Apocalyptic Visions in Contemporary America*, Berkeley: University of California Press, 2006

Richard Beck, *We Believe the Children: A Moral Panic in the 1980s*, New York: PublicAffairs, 2015

Paul H. Blaney, Robert F. Kruger, and Millon Theodore, *Oxford Textbook of Psychopathology*, New York: Oxford University Press, 2008

Daniel Burston, *A Forgotten Freudian: The Passion of Karl Stern*, New York: Routledge, 2018

Dan Herbeck and Lou Michel, *American Terrorist: Timothy McVeigh and the Oklahoma City Bombing*, New York: Harper, 2001

Annie Jacobsen, *Operation Paperclip: The Secret Intelligence Program that Brought Nazi Scientists to America*, New York: Little, Brown and Company, 2014

Mark Jacobson, *Pale Horse Rider: William Cooper, the Rise of Conspiracy, and the Fall of Trust in America*, New York: Blue Rider Press, 2018

Paul Krassner, *Murder at the Conspiracy Convention and other American Absurdities*, Fort Lee, NJ: Barricade Books, 2002

John Marks, *The Search for the Manchurian Candidate: The CIA and*

Mind Control, New York: Times Books, 1979

Alfred W. McCoy, *In the Shadows of the American Century: The Rise and Decline of US Global Power*, Chicago: Haymarket Books, 2017

—— *A Question of Torture: CIA Interrogation, from the Cold War to the War on Terror*, New York: Metropolitan Books, 2006

George Michael, *Lone Wolf Terror and the Rise of Leaderless Resistance*, Nashville: Vanderbilt University Press, 2012

Debbie Nathan, *Sybil Exposed: The Extraordinary Story Behind the Famous Multiple Personality Case*, New York: Free Press, 2011

Debbie Nathan and Michael Snedeker, *Satan's Silence: Ritual Abuse and the Making of a Modern American Witch Hunt*, San Jose: Author's Choice Press, 2001

Cathy O'Brien and Mark Phillips, *Trance:formation of America: The True Life Story of a Mind Control Slave*, Reality Marketing, 1995

Richard Ofshe and Ethan Watters, *Making Monsters: False Memories, Psychotherapy, and Sexual Hysteria*, Berkeley: University of California Press, 1996

Adam Parfrey, *Cult Rapture*, Portland, OR: Feral House, 1995

Mark Pendergrast, *Memory Warp: How the Myth of Repressed Memory Arose and Refuses to Die*, Hinsburg, VT: Upper Access Books, 2017

Colin A. Ross, M.D., *The C.I.A. Doctors: Human Rights Violations by American Psychiatrists*, Richardson, TX: Manitou Communications, 2006

—— *Military Mind Control: A Story of Trauma and Recovery*, Richardson, TX: Manitou Communications, 2009

—— *The Osiris Complex: Case Studies in Multiple Personality Disorder*, Toronto: University of Toronto Press, 1994

Flora Rheta Schreiber, *Sybil*, New York: Warner Paperback Library, 1974

Nicholas P. Spanos, *Multiple Identities & False Memories: A Sociocognitive Perspective*, Washington, D.C.: American Psychological Association, 2001

Jeffrey S. Victor, *Satanic Panic: The Creation of a Contemporary Legend*,

Chicago: Open Court Publishing Company, 1993
Robert Anton Wilson, *Cosmic Trigger I: Final Secret of the Illuminati*,
Tempe, Arizona: New Falcon, 2000

ARTICLES

Cynthia Hanson, "Dangerous Therapy: The Story of Patricia Burgus
and Multiple Personality Disorder," *Chicago,* June 1, 1998
Matt Keenan, "The Devil and Dr. Braun," *New City Chicago*, June 22-
28, 1995
Alexander Nazaryan, "Autism, Murder, and a Woman on the Ledge,"
Newsweek, October 19, 2014
Ann Zimmerman, "Cult of Madness," *Dallas Observer*, October, 1999

INTERVIEWS

H.P. Albarelli, April 18, 2018
Fabio, March 28, 2018
Lucien Greaves, April 16, 2018
Roma Hart, March 12, 2018
Roma Hart, May 18, 2018
Elizabeth Loftus, May 22, 2018
Colin Ross, March 9, 2018
Colin Ross, March 23, 2018
Colin Ross, July 19, 2018

NOTES

Where possible, I have included the sources as footnotes. In instances where this would be too unwieldy (when chapters were largely drawn from a couple sources, or from interviews that I've conducted) I include the sources below.

INTRODUCTION

1. http://www.zinewiki.com/Flipside
2. Wilson, *The Cosmic Trigger,* p. 6

SATAN GOES TO THE CONSPIRACY CONVENTION

Preface

3. *Historic Hotels of America,* National Trust for Historic Preservation. https://goo.gl/4fthKd
4. *DSM-IV,* p.477
5. Ofshe and Watters, *Making Monsters,* pg. 2
6. Anita Lipton, "Recovered Memories in the Courts," February 25, 2014. http://archive.fo/JPahv
7. Beck, *We Believe the Children,* p. *xxii*
8. Beck, *We Believe the Children,* p. 37
9. Beck, *We Believe the Children,* p. 154
10. Robert Reinhold, "The Longest Trial," *The New York Times,* January 24, 1990. http://archive.fo/w00x
11. Daphne L. Rankin, Virginia Commonwealth University http://archive.fo/exlaW
12. Barkun, *A Culture of Conspiracy,* pg. *x*
13. Herbeck and Michel, *American Terrorist: Timothy McVeigh and the Oklahoma City Bombing,* https://goo.gl/nHbsen
14. Alex Seitz-Wald, "Alex Jones: Conspiracy Inc.," *Salon,* May 2,

2013. http://archive.fo/9ASfU

15. Maxwell Tani and Michal Kranz,"18 outlandish conspiracy theories Donald Trump has floated on the campaign trail and in the White House," *Business Insider*, November 30, 2017. https://goo.gl/P8bzEB

16. Joseph L. Flatley, "James Tracy and the Boston Marathon bombing deniers," *Pando*, May 15, 2015. http://archive.fo/Ti8SN

17. Gianluca Mezzofiore and Justin Lear, "From 8chan to YouTube and Trump rallies: how a right-wing conspiracy theory is going mainstream," CNN, August 1, 2018. http://archive.fo/0Af9U

Chapter One

18. http://www.isst-d.org/default.asp?contentID=9

19. https://www.guidestar.org/profile/36-3465788

20. *Oxford Textbook of Psychopathology*, p. 456

21. Cynthia Hanson, "Dangerous Therapy: The Story of Patricia Burgus and Multiple Personality Disorder," *Chicago*, June 1, 1998. http://archive.fo/omtAS

22. Matt Keenan, "The Devil and Dr. Braun," *New City Chicago*, June 22-28, 1995. http://archive.fo/qXgQf

23. https://medicine.utah.edu/faculty/mddetail.php?facultyID=u0032313

24. The "Greenbaum Speech," http://archive.li/2r25n

25. Jacobsen, *Operation Paperclip*, pg. *ix*

26. Lawrence Patihis, Lavina Y. Ho, Ian W. Tingen, Scott O. Lilienfeld, Elizabeth F. Loftus, "Are the 'Memory Wars' Over? A Scientist-Practitioner Gap in Beliefs About Repressed Memory Show," *Psychological Science* 2014, Vol. 25(2) pp. 519–530

27. Pendergrast, *Memory Warp*, pg. 14

28. William Reville, "Childhood trauma may lead to split personality," *The Irish Times*, January 26, 1998. https://goo.gl/rwUH6g

29. Schreiber, *Sybil*, pp. 11-12

30. Author interview with Colin Ross (March 9, 2018)

31. https://www.nimh.nih.gov/health/statistics/schizophrenia.shtml
32. https://www.nimh.nih.gov/health/statistics/bipolar-disorder.shtml

Chapter Two

The main sources for this chapter are the books *Military Mind Control* by Colin Ross, *The Search for the Manchurian Candidate* by John Marks and a conversation with investigative journalist H.P. Albarelli.

33. McCoy, *A Question of Torture*, p. 28
34. Marks, *The Search for the Manchurian Candidate*, pp. 61-73
35. Ross, *Military Mind Control*, p. 64
36. O'Brien and Phillips, *Trance:formation of America*, p. 3
37. Barkun, *A Culture of Conspiracy,* p. 76
38. Fritz Springmeier, "Project Monarch: How the U.S. Creates Slaves of Satan," *A Newsletter from a Christian Ministry*, December 1993. Reprinted in Parfrey, *Cult Rapture* pp. 241-248
39. Author interview with Colin Ross (July 19, 2018) and http://www.prweb.com/releases/torture/cia/prweb2204544.htm
40. Burston, *A Forgotten Freudian*, https://goo.gl/bghrXa
41. H.A. Magnus, "Obituary Notices," *British Medical Journal* September 23, 1967, pp. 803–804
42. Marks, *The Search for the Manchurian Candidate,* p. 133
43. David Remnick, "25 Years of Nightmares," *The Washington Post*, July 28, 1985. https://goo.gl/sP3QHS
44. Clyde H. Farnsworth, "Canada Will Pay 50's Test Victims" *The New York Times*, November 19, 1992. http://archive.fo/hOXoe
45. Elizabeth Thompson, "Federal government quietly compensates daughter of brainwashing experiments victim," *CBC News*, October 26, 2017. http://archive.fo/3qOKA

Chapter Three

This chapter is largely drawn from conversations with Colin Ross and

Lucien Greaves, and from *Multiple Identities & False Memories: A Sociocognitive Perspective* by Nicholas P. Spanos.

46. Matt Miller, "Why the Satanic Temple Is Opening Its Doors to American Muslims," *Esquire*, November 21, 2015. https://goo.gl/p1w61f
47. Lee DeVito, "The Satanic Temple countered Planned Parenthood protests with some guerrilla theatre," *Detroit Metro Times*, August 24, 2015. http://archive.fo/jHGsC
48. Andrew Blake, "Satanic Temple offers help to Muslims amid post-Paris backlash," *The Washington Times*, November 19, 2015. http://archive.fo/YntTF
49. Adam Forrest, "Satanic temple sparks uproar by unveiling statue of goat-headed, winged creature called Baphomet in Arkansas state capitol," *Independent* (UK), August 17, 2018. http://archive.fo/QaFBK
50. Robert A. Baker, "In Memoriam: Nick Spanos." *Skeptical Inquirer*, Fall 1994
51. Spanos, *Multiple Identities and False Memories* p. 231
52. http://www.palmerhousehiltonhotel.com/press/palmer-house-backgrounder/

Chapter Four

This chapter largely draws on my interview with *Fabio*, the pseudonymous ISST-D whistleblower. The stuff about Sybil comes from the book *Sybil Exposed* by Debbie Nathan.

53. Debbie Nathan, "A Girl Not Named Sybil," *New York Times Magazine*, October 14, 2011. http://archive.fo/vhFUM

Chapter Five

Sources for this chapter include *The Osiris Complex* by Colin Ross;

Memory Warp: How the Myth of Repressed Memory Arose and Refuses to Die, by Mark Pendergrast; and the author's interview with Elizabeth Loftus, a memory researcher at the University of California, Irvine.

54. Linda Myer Williams, "Recall of Childhood Trauma: A Prospective Study of Women's Memories of Child Sexual Abuse," *Journal of Consulting and Clinical Psychology* 1994, vol. 62 no. 6, 1167-1176
55. Pendergrast, *Memory Warp*, pp. 78-9

Chapter Six

This chapter is based on several phone calls I had with Roma Hart between March and May 2018. Other sources for this chapter include an affidavit that Hart filed with the Manitoba Court of Queen's Bench requesting an extension of the statute of limitations (available at: http://archive.fo/E6EEs) and the collected affidavits and depositions of George Bergen (https://archive.org/details/EvidenceAgainstDr.ColinA.RossVol.1).

56. Affidavit of Roma Elizabeth Hart, February 27, 2004. http://archive.fo/E6EEs
57. Ross, *The Osiris Complex*, p. 148

Chapter Seven

In addition to reports in the *New York Daily News* and *New York Post*, this chapter is based on the transcripts of Jude Mirra's State of Wyoming shelter care hearing (available at: https://goo.gl/qnFPU2) as well as the article "Autism, Murder, and a Woman on the Ledge" by Alexander Nazaryan (*Newsweek*, October 19, 2014).

58. Rocco Parascandola, Kerry Burke, and Larry McShane, "Gigi

Jordan feeds son, 8, fatal dose of pills, leaves strange 2-page note in botched murder-suicide," *New York Daily News*, February 6, 2010. http://archive.fo/L2YmK

59. Rebecca Rosenberg, "Millionaire admits to 'mercy killing' of autistic son," *New York Post*, October 8, 2014. http://archive.fo/RDIy0

60. Bethania Palma Markus, "Mom murdered her autistic son after seeking help from therapist who believes in 'Satanic mind control,'" *Raw Story*, February 6, 2015. http://archive.fo/eyn7G

61. Rebecca Rosenberg, "Gigi's son had developed multiple personalities: shrink," *New York Post*, October 17, 2014. http://archive.fo/PZQcB

62. Eileen Avenni, who we met earlier, is also a former head of the ISST-D's Ritual Abuse/Mind Control/Organized Abuse Special Interest Group

63. Rebecca Rosenberg, "Millionaire mom who killed autistic son gets 18 years in jail," *New York Post*, May 28, 2015. http://archive.fo/7yP7F

Chapter Eight

This chapter largely draws from two sources: the author's interview of Colin Ross, and the story "Cult of Madness" by Ann Zimmerman (*Dallas Observer*, October, 1999).

64. Pendergrast, *Memory Warp*, p. 365

65. "Interview with Ms. Roma E. Hart by Douglas Mesner," April 7, 2016. http://archive.fo/ec6tq

66. The episode is titled "False Memory Syndrome." https://www.imdb.com/title/tt5830390/

Chapter Nine

67. Faiz Siddiqui and Susan Svrluga, "N.C. man told police he went to D.C. pizzeria with gun to investigate conspiracy theory,"

Washington Post, December 5, 2016. http://archive.fo/7hfqK

68. Amanda Robb, "Pizzagate: Anatomy of a Fake News Scandal," *Rolling Stone*, November 16, 2017. https://goo.gl/guCaiH

69. Merrit Kennedy, "'Pizzagate' Gunman Sentenced To 4 Years In Prison," *NPR*, June 22, 2017. http://archive.li/GqWTr

70. Adam Goldman, "The Comet Ping Pong Gunman Answers Our Reporter's Questions," *The New York Times*, December 7, 2016. http://archive.li/AISKA

71. Lawrence Patihis and Mark H. Pendergrast, "Reports of Recovered Memories of Abuse in Therapy in a Large Age-Representative U.S. National Sample: Therapy Type and Decade Comparisons," *Clinical Psychological Science*, May 31, 2018

72. Victor, *Satanic Panic,* p. 55

73. Victor, *Satanic Panic,* p. 56

...AND OTHER STORIES

The Rise of the Conspiracy Creeps

74. Alex Seitz-Wald, "Alex Jones: Conspiracy Inc.," *Salon*, May 2, 2013. http://archive.fo/9ASfU

The Boston Marathon Bombing 'Truth' Movement

75. Alexander Abad-Santos, "Good News: Boston's Man in the Chair Is Doing Great — and Boston's on Its Way," *The Atlantic*, April 24, 2013. https://goo.gl/iYKt3P

76. In May 2015, the jury sentenced Tsarnaev to death on six counts, "in a unanimous decision by the jury after 14 hours of deliberation." according to *The Guardian* http://archive.fo/aJ9JJ

77. Brian MacQuarrie, "Spectator's picture of scene draws attention," *Boston Globe*, April 18, 2013.http://archive.fo/P6maV

The Moon Is Its Own Light

78. Brian Dunning, "The Flat Earth Theory," *Skeptoid* Nov. 27, 2012. http://archive.fo/ChheP
79. "Everything is fake: Top 40 pieces of fakery in our World," *Intellihub*, 8/14/15. http://archive.fo/hdGTP

The Conspiracy Entrepreneur

80. "Top 6 Climate Change Problems," March 12, 2015. https://youtu.be/4Ew05sRDAcU

The Targeted Individuals

81. Robert Guffey, "To See the Invisible Man," *UFO Magazine*, March 2007.
82. Glenn Greenwald and Betsy Reed, "Secret Docs Reveal: President Trump Has Inherited an FBI with Vast Hidden Powers," *The Intercept*, Jan. 31, 2017. http://archive.fo/IHA0B

EPILOGUE

83. "Names of deceased victims in Squirrel Hill massacre released," *Pittsburgh Post-Gazette*, October 28, 2018. http://archive.fo/tLHRD
84. "Pittsburgh Synagogue Massacre Suspect Was 'Pretty Much a Ghost,'" *The New York Times*, October 28, 2018. http://archive.fo/SQoeW
85. Jessica McBride, "Robert Bowers: See Squirrel Hill Suspect's Social Media," *Heavy*. http://archive.fo/7pJgk
86. "The Pittsburgh synagogue shooting is believed to be the deadliest attack on Jews in American history, the ADL says," *CNN*, October 28, 2018. http://archive.fo/uE0zW
87. United States of America vs. Robert Bowers Criminal Complaint, Case No. 18-1396

88. "A high school dropout and trucker, Robert Bowers left few footprints—except online," *Pittsburgh Post Gazette*, October 29, 2018. https://goo.gl/t1sa8x

89. Alex Amend, "Analyzing a terrorist's social media manifesto: the Pittsburgh synagogue shooter's posts on Gab," *Hatewatch*, October 28, 2018. https://goo.gl/MbKRvk

90. Michael, *Lone Wolf Terror and the Rise of Leaderless Resistance*, p. 42

91. Chip Berlet, "Heroes Know Which Villains to Kill: How Coded Rhetoric Incites Scripted Violence," https://goo.gl/PFfdmC

92. Chip Berlet, "How the Rhetoric of Right-Wing Populism with its 'Producerist' Conspiracy Theories Fuels a Bigoted Right-Wing Juggernaut Promoting White Nationalism" https://goo.gl/sK17Z6

93. "From nonpartisan voter to virulent extremist: The undoing of Robert Bowers," *Pittsburgh Post-Gazette*, http://archive.fo/DNLaa

94. Alex Amend, "Analyzing a terrorist's social media manifesto: the Pittsburgh synagogue shooter's posts on Gab," *Hatewatch*, October 28, 2018. https://goo.gl/MbKRvk

95. Turkay Salim Nefes, "How conspiracy theories feed political fragmentation," June 29, 2017. http://archive.fo/QvIqa

96. Richard Gonzales, "Trump Says He'll Send As Many As 15,000 Troops To The Southern Border," *NPR*, October 31, 2018. http://archive.fo/ZTFwp

97. Vivian Lee, "Pittsburgh Synagogue Shooting: Questions and Anomalies," *The Memory Hole Blog*, October 29, 2018. http://archive.fo/fQsKp

98. Mark Jacobson, *Pale Horse Rider*, pg. 160

99. Scott Harris, "Spreading Hate and Fear, Trump Incites Far Right Terrorism," *Between the Lines*, October 31, 2018. https://goo.gl/GFj567

100. "Who is Cesar Sayoc? What we know about the suspected mail bomber arrested in Florida," *Washington Post*, October 26, 2018. https://goo.gl/sU1WCq

101. David Ludden Ph.D., "Why Do People Believe in Conspiracy Theories?" *Psychology Today Blogs*, January 6, 2018.

http://archive.fo/V8sSw
102. Christopher French, "Why Do Some People Believe in Conspiracy Theories?" *Scientific American*, June 11, 2015. http://archive.fo/xSYSC
103. Josh Gabbatiss, "Scientists discover the reason people believe in conspiracy theories," *Independant*, August 20, 2018. http://archive.fo/72WR8
104. Paul Musgrave, "Conspiracy theories are for losers. QAnon is no exception," *Washington Post*, August 2, 2018. https://goo.gl/Qo1B3y
105. Domenico Montanaro, "Here's Just How Little Confidence Americans Have In Political Institutions,' *NPR*, January 17, 2018. http://archive.fo/Lw80E
106. "Pittsburgh Mayor Bill Peduto leads his city through its darkest days," *Washington Post*, November 3, 2018. https://goo.gl/jmMza8
107. "Trump says Pittsburgh synagogue should have had armed guards," *CNN*, October 28, 2018. https://goo.gl/3wu5X5
108. "Here's the 'small protest' Trump says he didn't see in Pittsburgh," *Washington Post*, October 31, 2018. https://goo.gl/zk247m